Album of My Life

A MEMOIR

Album of My Life
Ann Szedlecki

The Azrieli Foundation
164 Eglinton Avenue East, Suite 503
Toronto, Ontario
Canada, M4P 1G4
www.azrielifoundation.org

Cover and book design by Mark Goldstein
Cartography by Karen van Kerkoele

Library and Archives Canada Cataloguing in Publication

Szedlecki, Ann, 1925–2005
    Album of my life / Ann Szedlecki.

(Azrieli series of Holocaust survivor memoirs. Series II)
Includes bibliographical references and index.
ISBN 978-1-897470-10-7

1. Szdelecki, Ann, 1925–2005. 2. Holocaust, Jewish (1939–1945) – Poland. 3. Jewish children in the Holocaust – Poland – Biography. 4. Jews – Poland – Biography. 5. Jews – Soviet Union – Biography. I. Azrieli Foundation II. Title. III. Series: Azrieli series of Holocaust survivor memoirs. Series II

D804.196.S94 2009   940.53'18092   C2009-901396-7

Printed in Canada

The Azrieli Series of Holocaust Survivor Memoirs

Contents

Series Preface:
In their own words...

In telling these stories, the writers have liberated themselves. For so many years we did not speak about it, even when we became free people living in a free society. Now, when at last we are writing about what happened to us in this dark period of history, knowing that our stories will be read and live on, it is possible for us to feel truly free. These unique historical documents put a face on what was lost, and allow readers to grasp the enormity of what happened to six million Jews – one story at a time.

David J. Azrieli, C.M., C.Q., MArch
Holocaust survivor and founder, The Azrieli Foundation

Since the end of World War II, over 30,000 Jewish Holocaust survivors have immigrated to Canada. Who they are, where they came from, what they experienced and how they built new lives for themselves and their families are important parts of our Canadian heritage. The Azrieli Foundation-York University Holocaust Survivor Memoirs Program was established to preserve and share the memoirs written by those who survived the twentieth-century Nazi genocide of the Jews of Europe and later made their way to Canada. The program is guided by the conviction that each survivor of the Holocaust has a remarkable story to tell, and that such stories play an important role in education about tolerance and diversity.

Millions of individual stories are lost to us forever. By preserving the stories written by survivors and making them widely available to a broad audience, the Azrieli Series of Holocaust Survivor Memoirs seeks to sustain the memory of all those who perished at the hands of hatred, abetted by indifference and apathy. The personal accounts of those who survived against all odds are as different as the people who wrote them, but all demonstrate the courage, strength, wit and luck that it took to prevail and survive in such terrible adversity. The memoirs are also moving tributes to people – strangers and friends – who risked their lives to help others, and who, through acts of kindness and decency in the darkest of moments, frequently helped the persecuted maintain faith in humanity and courage to endure. These accounts offer inspiration to all, as does the survivors' desire to share their experiences so that new generations can learn from them.

The Holocaust Survivor Memoirs Program collects, archives and publishes these distinctive records and the print editions are available free of charge to libraries, schools and Holocaust-education programs across Canada, and to the general public at Azrieli Foundation educational events. Online editions of the books are available on our web site, www.azrielifoundation.org.

The Israel and Golda Koschitzky Centre for Jewish Studies has provided scholarly assistance and guidance in the preparation of these memoirs for publication. The manuscripts as originally submitted are preserved in the Clara Thomas Archives and Special Collections at York University, and are available for review by interested scholars.

The Azrieli Foundation would like to express deep appreciation to Tamarah Feder, Managing Editor and Program Manager 2005–2008 for her contribution to the establishment of this program and for her work on Series I and II. The program also gratefully acknowledges the following people for their invaluable efforts in producing this series: Mary Arvanitakis, Elin Beaumont, François Blanc, Aurélien Bonin, Florence Buathier, Mark Celinscack, Nicolas Côté, Darrel Dickson (Maracle Press), Andrea Geddes Poole, Sir Martin Gilbert, Esther Goldberg, Mark Goldstein, Irena Kohn, Elizabeth Lasserre, Lisa Newman, Carson Phillips, Susan Roitman, Judith Samuels, Randall Schnoor, Erica Simmons, Jody Spiegel, Mia Spiro, Erika Tucker and Karen Van Kerkoerle.

Introduction

There are people you get to know on the pages of a book whom you wish you could meet in person. So it is with Ann Szedlecki. In the compelling memoir you are about to read, Ann begins by calling herself "the daughter of nobody," someone with a past that has "disappeared." And yet, as she draws us into the life she led as a girl and young woman during World War II, she brings this past to life. Accompanying her on a long journey from her happy childhood in pre-war Poland to the cold harshness of Siberia, from skipping along Lodz's streets dreaming of ice-cream to walking the route of a Soviet postal carrier in Ust-Kamenogorsk, we are drawn to this courageous, resilient, warm and funny woman. Ann Szedlecki's highly readable story of wartime survival and coming-of age is full of rich detail and poignant observation, beautifully rendering the vicissitudes of one young woman's life in relation to the large-scale historical events that helped shape its course.

Ann Szedlecki was born Chana Frajlich in Lodz in 1925, the youngest child of Shimshon and Liba Bayla Frajlich. She begins her story by deftly reconstructing scenes from her pre-war childhood in the impoverished Jewish neighbourhood of Lodz, recounting the details of everyday life by invoking the image of an album of memories, inviting the reader to open it up with her, page by page. The author lovingly describes her parents and close relatives, musing on their characters and bringing out their personalities. Ann's superbly executed portraits of the characters that peopled her world – the housewives, bakers, tailors, acrobats and undertakers – are tender and humourous, infused with a deep appreciation of Yiddish language and culture as well as the grief-tinged knowledge that this is a vanished world and way of life. Ann's is also the story of an ordinary girl growing up – a girl who loved music and the movies, swimming and skating, and whose sense of self and place was very strong. Her family was poor and made even poorer by the onset of the Depression, but she was secure in the embrace of loving, caring people and in her identity as a Jew in Poland in the interwar period.

In 1939 Poland had the largest Jewish population of any country in Europe – approximately 3.3 million. The Jewish community in Poland had flourished for centuries and, in comparison to elsewhere in Eastern Europe and Russia, Polish Jews had experienced relatively peaceful relations with their neighbours. The Jews of Poland were able to develop important religious and national movements, establish renowned centres of religious learning, and develop the rich cultural heritage of the Yiddish language – the daily language of Eastern European Jews. By the middle of the twentieth century, Polish Jews had created a distinctive literary tradition that included Yiddish fiction, poetry, theatre and cinema. Life for the Jewish community of Poland was one also one of conflict and discrimination, however, its members often subject to prejudice and persecution and even physical assault by their non-Jewish neighbours. Jews had long been accepted because the commercial and financial activities they engaged in were seen to be beneficial to the economic life of the country, but long-standing religious bigotry endured and sometimes erupted with violent hostility.

The contradictions inherent in Jewish life in Poland became sharper in the interwar period. As a result of the post–World War I settlement, Poland became an independent country after more than a century of partition and rule by Russia, Prussia and Austria. Polish nationalism, growing since the end of the nineteenth century, now surged and also touched the Jewish population, who increasingly and proudly took part in the country's political life and in outward expressions of nationalist support. The leadership of Marshal Josef Piłsudski – the father of the interwar Second Polish Republic – was largely viewed positively by the Jewish community. His policy of "state assimilation," whereby citizens were judged not by their ethnicity but by their loyalty to the state, was seen as a great improvement over prior official attitudes. In addition, as Poland modernized and urban centres grew, many professions and industries became less restrictive, and opportunities for Jews opened up. Yet at the same time, and especially in the latter half of the 1930s, the rise in nationalist sentiment led to growing intolerance of ethnic minority groups by the general population and Jews, among others, found themselves the target of discriminatory practices. With the impact of the worldwide economic Great Depression that began in the early 1930s, the condition of Polish Jews steadily worsened.

Poland's Jewish community was increasingly urbanized and by the early twentieth century the majority of the population – Ann's parents among them – had moved from small towns and villages to cities. Polish Jews were also influenced by the process of modernization taking place all over Europe. Most Jews were very observant in their religious practice – what we would call Orthodox today – but many also tried to embrace traditional ways while also pursuing secular learning. Still others began to move away from traditional religious practice and looked for other political or cultural ways to define themselves as Jews. For some, a person's comfort level in Polish, as opposed to Yiddish, became a signifier of how progressive and modern they were. Ann's family presented a microcosm of these trends: while her father began to wear modern clothing once he moved to Lodz he was nonetheless extremely pious and spoke only Yiddish; her religiously observant mother, on the other hand, spoke Polish fluently, read all the newspapers and partook of Lodz's exciting cultural scene. Moving to the next generation, her older sister and brother often ignored religious observances altogether and took an interest in the political and ideological debates of the day. Ann's school for Jewish girls included religious instruction, but the classes were conducted entirely in Polish.

The trends influencing Poland as a whole were also apparent in Lodz, the city Ann's family called home. Located approximately seventy-five miles southwest of Warsaw, Lodz was an industrial city with a Jewish population of about 233,000 on the eve of the war, roughly one-third of the total. Prior to World War II, the Jewish community in Lodz was the second largest Europe. Known as the "Manchester of Poland," Lodz was famous for its textile industry and Jews played an important role in it – the ready-made tailoring industry was almost entirely made up of Jews, among them Ann's father. Jews were also active as merchants, traders and builders and several wealthy Jewish families from Lodz were well-known throughout Poland. Lodz had a varied and vibrant religious, social, cultural and political scene. And yet, the Jewish community was still largely separate from the Polish population as a whole and the reader is struck by how sheltered young Ann's life was before the war. Leaving Lodz in late 1939 at the age of fourteen, Ann takes note of the fact that until then she had been surrounded almost exclusively by Jews.

The pre-war world of Jewish Lodz, so evocatively conjured up in Ann's vignettes, was shattered in the fall of 1939. On September 1, Germany invaded Poland and one week later occupied Lodz. The Germans renamed the city Litzmannstadt and incorporated it into the Third Reich. The consequences for the Jewish community were immediate: harsh measures were imposed to strip Jews of all legal, economic and social rights. Among other things, Jewish property was confiscated, Jews were not allowed in public parks, many Jews were forbidden to continue in their jobs or professions, and Jews were forced to wear a visible marker on their clothing identifying them as Jews. Daily roundups of Jews for forced labour began, as well as random beatings and killings on the streets. In February 1940, the Germans established a ghetto in the northeast part of Lodz – a restricted area for Jews who could not live anywhere else in the city. The Lodz ghetto soon became the second largest in Poland, after Warsaw. After May 1, 1940, the Lodz ghetto was also the most hermetically sealed, with its 200,000 residents working in terrible and dehumanizing conditions as slaves providing supplies for the German army.

Although Ann experienced the beginning of the Nazis' persecution in Lodz, she did not stay in the city long enough to see the ghetto established. Instead, at the end of November 1939, she joined her twenty-year-old brother Shoel and left Lodz, heading east for Soviet-occupied territory. In this they were not alone: between September 30, 1939, and May 1, 1940, 70,000 Jews left Lodz, the great majority heading in an easterly direction in the belief that life would be better in the areas now controlled by the USSR. Most intended to wait out what they hoped would be a short war until things settled down. The Soviet Union controlled the eastern half of Poland under the terms of an agreement signed with the Nazis in August 1939 known as the Molotov-Ribbentrop Pact. Ann's parents refused to leave, insisting on staying with their eldest daughter who had an infant to care for and who was awaiting news of her husband – he had not been seen since his mobilization into the Polish army in late August 1939. Clearly worried enough about what the future might hold to let her youngest child leave, Ann later came to see her mother's decision as "the highest maternal sacrifice and act of deep love."

It is one of the stark truths of the Holocaust that the events and choices that led to the survival of one person could mean death for another. Throughout her journey, Ann was faced with choices about where to go and what to do, and almost every time she made one, or had one imposed on her, it ultimately worked in her favour. Yet it could so easily have gone the other way. In her case the decision to separate from her family ultimately saved her, but it was the experience of many other survivors that families that stayed together found greater opportunities for survival. One cannot help but be struck by the arbitrariness of life under conditions of total war and the Nazis' organized, murderous persecution. We are also left with a deep sense of the gnawing questions that remain when survivors do not even know of the choices faced by their loved ones and what happened to them. After November 1939, Ann never saw her family again and she knew no details about what happened to them or when and where they died. It was a mystery that she was never able to solve and that weighed on her for the rest of her life. She was able to ascertain only that her family somehow ended up in the Warsaw ghetto rather than in Lodz, and she suspected that they were deported from there to their deaths in the summer of 1942.

Ann knew nothing of what was to come, for her family in Lodz or for herself and Shoel, and though she felt fear and trepidation as she headed east she also felt excitement. She was, after all, a fourteen-year-old girl leaving home for the first time. With no knowledge of the horrors the war would bring, Ann felt that she was embarking on an adventure. Arriving in Bialystok and finding tens of thousands of other refugees living in terrible conditions, Ann and her brother were soon faced with the choice of taking on Soviet citizenship and staying in Soviet-occupied territory, going back to German-occupied Poland, or volunteering to work in remote areas of the USSR under a special Soviet program that was meant to simultaneously solve the growing refugee problem in their newly occupied territories and assist the Soviet economy. Ann and Shoel decided to volunteer, one example of a fateful decision that led to her survival. In a cruel twist of fate, this same decision ended up being a death sentence for her brother.

Leaving Bialystok in January 1940 with an official transport of Polish refugee volunteers, Ann and her brother made a 4,500-kilometre trek across the Ural Mountains and eventually reached the town of Ridder in northeastern Kazakhstan. For the next six and a half years, Ridder (renamed Leninogorsk in 1941) and the smaller town of Ust-Kamenogorsk would be her home. She quickly learned Russian and at first was even able to continue her education, but life in this remote, cold outpost was soon one of hunger, fear, loss and a profound and pervasive loneliness. Her life in Siberia was filled with relentless hardship, including six months in a hard-labour camp where she was sent for the crime of being absent from work without permission. She committed this terrible offence in order to bury her beloved brother. The weight and pain of Ann's grief over Shoel, who died in 1943 at twenty-three, was matched by her feelings of guilt that she was not with her brother when he died. Yet she also remembers the adventures, the stolen moments of warmth, friendship, luck and even fun. And she acknowledges with particular feeling the kindness of strangers, including many non-Jews, who became friends and who helped give her the sense of belonging and safety that she craved – especially her beloved Aunt Katia, a Ukrainian exile who eventually took her in.

Ann's powerful and vivid depiction of her life in Siberia offers a window into a part of the Holocaust that has remained relatively unexplored – that is, the world of European Jews who escaped to what was then the Soviet Union. From the time the Nazis invaded Poland in September 1939 until they launched their attack on the USSR in June 1941, nearly 10 per cent of the Jewish population of Poland – some 300,000 Jews – fled German-occupied areas of Poland and crossed into the Soviet zone. Although it is impossible to know for sure, it is estimated that more than half of this number stayed in the USSR, some moving more deeply into the Soviet Union. During this same period Soviet authorities sought to "Sovietize" the formerly Polish territories they now occupied – which is to say, to impose their social, political and economic structure and remove any capitalist, bourgeois or other threatening tendencies. As a result, tens of thousands of Jews and others were deported to Siberia, Central Asia and other remote areas in the interior of the Soviet Union on various political and ideologically motivated charges. Finally, after Hitler turned his army against his erstwhile Soviet ally in June 1941, more than a million Soviet Jews and refugees from other countries fled eastward, many into the Asian parts of the country. Although exact numbers are hard to come by, experts believe that the Jews who escaped into the USSR, and especially those who were not located in the areas of German occupation after June 1941, constitute the largest group of European Jews to survive the Holocaust. Many Jews died under harsh and inhumane conditions, yet as cruel as life was under Stalin, escape and deportation to remote areas of the USSR ultimately saved Jewish lives.

The experiences of these USSR-based survivors remain under-studied in contrast to other aspects of the Holocaust, largely because Soviet sources were unavailable in the post-war period and because official Soviet policy was to ignore the specificities of the Jewish experience during World War II. Ann's skillful descriptions of life in wartime Siberia thus offer important insight into the lives and deaths of those who fled into the Soviet Union, and in particular into the diversity and variety of these stories. The population of the major towns in Siberia swelled in the period between 1941 and 1945 – with Jewish and non-Jewish refugees from East European countries, but also with Soviet citizens of many different ethnic backgrounds from all over the USSR. This latter group included both people who were evacuated or deported behind the Urals and worked in heavy industrial enterprises to support the war effort and, of course, prisoners serving time in forced-labour camps for a myriad of usually false charges.

Ann's observations also offer a window into the conflicted feelings of many Jewish refugees who survived in the Soviet Union. The conditions were terrible and often violent, yet this was better than the unthinkable fate they had left behind. Reflecting on her months of hard labour, she observes, "When I think of the poor victims of the concentration camps, we were well looked after in comparison." Many refugees and deportees felt grateful appreciation for their country of refuge, even though life under Stalin's dictatorship included arbitrary and ideological terror, violence and privation. Perhaps most importantly, Ann never experienced discrimination as a Jew in the Soviet Union – rather, Soviet authorities were equally brutal toward all their citizens. As she wrote, "I was hungry, homeless, dirty and friendless, but none of that was because of who or what I was. We all shared a common misery in the Soviet Union." And yet, in the very next paragraph, she can't help pointing out that horses were frequently treated better than people, as when prisoners were called out to haul firewood during severe snowstorms rather than the usual horses who were kept safe and warm in their stables. As always, Ann shows her humour and grace while looking back on her experience of hard labour: "Before my imprisonment I ate only every second or third day. The camp really spoiled me – they fed me three times a day!"

Ann's candid account of the experiences of women during the war is also notable. Throughout the memoir, she notes the numerous instances in which male acquaintances tried to manipulate a promise of aid into payment by sexual favours. We witness her luck and skill in averting unwanted outcomes, as well as the more prosaic and daily difficulties of being a woman under these conditions. In addition, she offers observations of the home front in the USSR that are not often found in English-language sources. She describes the hardships and changes in daily life due to the war, but also how life went on regardless: people worked and went to school, got married and had babies, put on theatre productions and went to the movies … and the mail was still delivered, eventually by Ann herself when she got a job as a letter carrier.

The contributions of this memoir to our understanding of the varied Jewish experiences during World War II are significant. However it is Ann Szedlecki's writing – full of rich detail, affecting and sensorial observations, and emblematic images – that stay with the reader after the pages have been turned: the beauty of a bent candlestick, never straightened, that come to represent her Uncle Hersh's jealousy over her sister's marriage; the overpowering smells of her childhood neighbourhood and of the camel-hair sweaters she knitted to support herself in Siberia; her descriptions of the extreme beauty of her surroundings while doing forced labour in freezing conditions. Throughout the memoir, the symbol of shoes recurs. From her first attempt at teen independence when she insists on heels instead of black-patent flats, to the joy of getting soft warm felt boots when she begins her favourite job as a Soviet postal worker in Siberia, Ann's footwear serve to represent where she was in her life.

Ann felt an inner sense of conflict over roots and wings that permeates the memoir. She needed to walk, wander and be free of constraints, but she always came up against her equally strong need to connect with her community after losing everyone and everything she held dear. Ann's exploration of her life as a wandering "hobo" focuses attention on an important aspect of her survival instinct – guided by a sense of inner liberty, Ann never gave in to despair during the war. Indeed, throughout this memoir one is struck not only by Ann's resilience and will, but by her inherent optimism and decency. As she made her way – young and alone, facing terrible conditions and choices – she was guided by the hope that she would see her family again and the promise she made to her mother the last time she saw her to "be decent." While Ann keeps this promise under the most challenging of circumstances, she does so in a world where most others are not guided by the same moral code. It is clear that Ann's optimism and strong moral centre is the key to her sense of self-respect and, in many ways, the strength that she was able to draw on to survive.

After the war, Ann returned to Lodz only to find no trace of her family or the life she had known before. When the Red Army liberated Lodz in January 1945 the city's Jewish population, once the second largest in Europe, numbered only nine hundred and the Jewish areas of the city had been destroyed. The rest of the city was in relatively good shape, especially in comparison to flattened, decimated Warsaw, and in the immediate post-war years, Lodz was something of a magnet for Jews returning to Poland. In 1946, the Jewish population of the city grew to 20,000. The Jews who came back included those who had spent the war in hiding with the help of forged identity papers and those who had survived Nazi camps. But by far the largest number of returnees to the city came from the thousands of Polish Jews from the Soviet Union – Ann among them – who were repatriated as part of an official program. For Ann, the return was a devastating experience. The hope that she had nurtured throughout her six and a half years was crushed and the inner sense of loneliness she had carried around since Shoel's death became ever more profound. At the age of twenty-one, she was completely and utterly alone. She was shocked, moreover, by the "welcome" she received: almost immediately upon setting foot on Polish soil she witnessed a violent antisemitic attack on another returning refugee.

Ann ended her memoir with her return to Lodz and made a conscious decision not to write about the events of her life after that. This is the case with many survivors who write memoirs and speaks to the fact that even after they have built new lives and the past recedes, the the war remains the seminal shaping event of their lives. Ann lost everyone and everything in her teen years, when her identity as an adult woman was taking shape, and her decision to explore only those years says much about the scars that never healed. And yet as readers we want to know what happened to this strong and lonely, plucky and ironically humourous young woman. After accompanying her on her journey to this point, it is natural to ask: what happened next?

Very soon after Ann returned to Lodz she met and married a man eleven years her senior, Abraham Szedlecki. According to the couple's daughter, Lynda Kraar, Abraham Szedlecki was originally from Konskie and had been incarcerated in the Lodz ghetto; he was deported to a labour camp in 1942 and eventually to Auschwitz. He was tall and handsome and apparently resembled Ann's brother, Shoel. Desperately searching for some kind of connection to hold on to, Ann fell for him as soon as she set eyes on him and the couple quickly married. Ann never dwelt on her marriage, but it did not turn out to be a happy one. Abraham Szedlecki was a broken spirit. He had lost a beloved pregnant wife during the war and was, according to his daughter, a "wounded, traumatized and sad guy." Ann was not able to fill her void of emptiness with him. And yet the two stayed married until Ann's death in May 2005, making two international moves together – from Poland to Israel in 1950 and to Canada in 1953 – putting down roots in Toronto and raising their daughter who was born in 1959. Abraham Szedlecki died in September 2007.

Although her marriage was less than ideal, Ann embraced her new life in Toronto. She began by working in the garment district sewing buttons, but quickly moved up to become a bookkeeper and eventually opened her own successful ladies clothing store, which she operated for twenty-five years. She became an avid community volunteer and never lost her love of the movies and music. Her deep core of loneliness was always present, but it was balanced by the humour, optimism and decency that were the mainstays of her wartime survival.

For a long time after the war, Ann maintained that she wasn't "really a Holocaust survivor" because she had never been in a Nazi camp and she was reluctant to talk about it. Over the years she shared her story with her daughter and then, in the mid-1990s, she began to talk about her experiences to school groups visiting the Toronto Holocaust Centre. She soon discovered that her natural talent as a storyteller could not only move but also educate people. She became a powerful and popular speaker and she decided to try her hand at writing.

Ann's discovery late in her life that she could write, and write well, was transformative for her. This is the case for many survivors for whom writing of the past becomes a kind of second liberation. The knowledge that the people, places and events of their lives will be preserved and the hope that someone will read and remember them after they are gone, is felt as both a relief and a release. Ann's memoir is significant for its literary merit, for its fidelity to historical detail and as a reminder of the diversity of Jewish experiences during the Nazi genocide. It is a remarkable testament to one woman's courage, decency and inner sense of freedom and to her loved ones from a lost world never to be forgotten.

Naomi Azrieli

2009

The author would like to thank and acknowledge Tamarah Feder and Irena Kohn for their unpublished 2006 abstract of *Album of My Life* that was used as a source for this introduction.

SOURCES:

Bender, Sara. *The Jews of Bialystok During World War II and the Holocaust.* Translated by Yaffa Murciano. Waltham, Massachusetts: Brandeis University Press, 2008.

Dabrowska, Danuta and Abraham Wein, eds. *Encyclopaedia of the Jewish Communities of Poland.* Volume I, "Lodz and its region." (Translation of *Pinkas hakehillot Polin: entsiklopedyah shel ha-yishuvim ha-Yehudiyim le-min hivasdam ve-`ad le-ahar Sho'at Milhemet ha-`olam ha-sheniyah*). Jerusalem: Yad Vashem, 1976. http://www.jewishgen.org/yizkor/pinkas_poland/pol1_00005.html#7

Dunphy, Catherine. "Ann Szedlecki, 79: 'Nobody's daughter' Spoke Up," *Toronto Star*, Obituaries, October 4, 2005.

Horowitz, Sara R. "Introduction" to Henia Reinhartz, *Bits and Pieces.* Toronto: The Azrieli Foundation, 2007.

Levin, Nora. *The Jews in the Soviet Union since 1917.* Volumes I and II. New York and London: New York University Press, 1988.

Mendelsohn, Ezra. "Jewish Politics in Interwar Poland: An Overview," in *The Jews of Poland Between Two World Wars,* ed. Yisrael Gutman. Hanover, New Hampshire: University Press of New England, 1989.

Mendelsohn, Ezra and Isaiah Trunk, eds. "Poland," in *Encyclopaedia Judaica*, 2nd Edition, Vol, 16. Ed., Fred Skolnik. New York: MacMillan, 2006.

Ro'i Ya'akov, ed. *Jews and Jewish Life in Russia and the Soviet Union.* Oxford: Taylor and Francis, 1995.

Rozett, Robert and Shmuel Spector, eds. *Encyclopedia of the Holocaust.* Jerusalem: Yad Vashem and The Jerusalem Publishing House, 2000.

Foreword

There was a taboo, noirish quip that some of us kids of Holocaust survivors heard as we were growing up: Hitler was the *shadchan* (matchmaker). It referred to the loveless marriages, the lifetimes of grief, anxiety and nightmares experienced by our parents. Today they have a name for it: post-traumatic stress disorder. However, this is a mere label, because there can be no mistake – our parents did not live in the "post-" world. Every day the act of waking up and getting out of bed was an excruciating experience that reminded them of their losses and refreshed the memories.

Despite all the love that they gave us, we kids felt a need to care for our parents, to shelter them from the world in which we were maturing. Yet, who had seen more than they had? We were naïve and innocent in our mission to protect our parents. We were, however, acutely aware that we, the next generation, could never replace the *kedoshim* – the martyrs – the families that were decimated during the war.

My mother was a complex person. In the course of writing her memoirs, over many years, she often talked to me about what would be omitted from her book and what would be included. She made a conscious decision to end her story with her return to Lodz and not delve into anything in her post-war life. And she also made a decision to exclude her husband – my father – from any mention in the story although she met and married him very soon after she returned to Lodz. She did so mainly because she met him after her story ends.

But it is also true that they did not have a happy life together. Although at first my father – older, tall and handsome – seemed like the perfect person for my young, romantic mother to build a new life with, it didn't work out that way. Under different circumstances, I was frequently told, they never would have met, let alone married. As it was, their life together was a tragic coexistence for two people who had suffered so much loss and who could have lived much happier, more fulfilling lives.

Like so many of the survivors, they left behind no last wishes with regard to their burial. At first I was seriously considering burying them apart so that they could break free from Hitler's unfortunate *shidduch* (match), but I realized that their fates were intertwined and the greatest tribute I could give them, as their sole survivor and for the sake of future generations, was to bury them next to each other.

~

My mother and I worked on this manuscript intermittently over the course of ten years. I'd help out when she asked me to type something up or to edit as she worked on the manuscript. After Mum became ill, I decided to spend more time with her. As long as her energy was good, I was able to transcribe and keep editing, asking questions as I went. There were several versions and I had to transcribe a lot of handwritten binder sheets along with some typed pages. After a collaboration of several months, Mum passed away on May 7, 2005, just three weeks shy of her eightieth birthday. I continued to work on the manuscript for more than a year. With Mum's voice silenced, I had to fend for myself and find new ways of getting my questions answered.

This book would not have been possible without the tutelage of Mum's memoir writing teacher, novelist Sylvia Warsh. For a decade my mother could not wait to get up on Friday mornings to attend Sylvia's class at the Betel Centre. My mum's surrogate daughter (and my best friend), Masha Starkman Ami, often served as a sounding board and secretary, usually on Tuesdays, when they would have lunch together at Mum's house.

My family and I are also grateful to the international community of members of the Kresy Siberia Discussion Group on yahoo.com and its founder, Stefan Wisniowski, for their help with translations, basic understanding of certain facts, and for sharing their own research and history on the various aspects of the Siberian experience for displaced Polish citizens. It was exhilarating to learn that Mum's story was helping to uncover a much larger historical narrative.

My family and I are grateful to Naomi Azrieli for fulfilling Mum's wish. I happened to be visiting Toronto on the fateful night when my friend Miriam Pilc-Levine invited me to a workshop on memoir writing at the Baycrest Centre during Holocaust Education Week in November 2005. It was during this workshop that Naomi Azrieli went to the podium and announced the Azrieli Foundation's Holocaust Survivor Memoirs Program. Miriam urged me to submit Mum's memoirs. That was the night I met Naomi and my mother's strong wish to have her memoirs published was fulfilled. It is bittersweet for our family. Growing up, I was well aware of my mother's powerful desire to bring her story to the public and to keep alive the memory of the world that she lost. Sadly, her race ended before she was able to see her life's work come to fruition. This book is all she ever really wanted. We are so proud of my mother's courage and dedication, and grateful to the Azrieli Foundation.

Lynda Kraar
2009

Ann's Family Tree*

PATERNAL GREAT GRANDMOTHER:
Sarah Frajlich
(maiden name unknown)
born 1830, died 1933 (at 103)

GRANDFATHER (father's father):
Kalmen Frajlich-Fajbusiak,
date of birth unknown

Married: first wife (Ann's grandmother) *Chana Rivka Frajlich*
(maiden name unknown);
second wife, last name *Fajbusiak,*
first name unknown)

FATHER:
Shimshon (haCohen) Frajlich;
born 1887 in or near Lodz

GRANDFATHER (mother's father):
Shoel Wajnert,
date of birth unknown

Married:
Miriam Chana Wajnert
(maiden name and date of birth
unknown)

MOTHER:
Liba Bayla (née *Wajnert*);
born 1886 in or near Lodz

BROTHER:
Shoel (haCohen) Frajlich;
born 1919 in Lodz

BROTHER:
Unknown

BROTHER:
Unknown

SISTER:
Malka ("Manya") Ceder
(née Frajlich); born 1916 in Lodz

Married:
Yoine ("Yanek") Ceder

NIECE:
Miriam Ceder
(Malka and Yoine's daughter);
born 1939 in Lodz

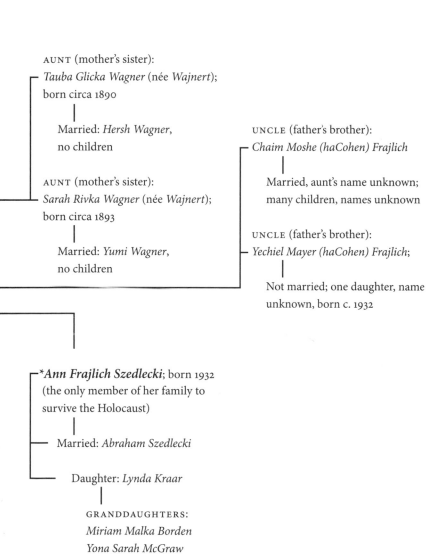

AUNT (mother's sister):
Tauba Glicka Wagner (née *Wajnert*);
born circa 1890

  Married: *Hersh Wagner*,
  no children

AUNT (mother's sister):
Sarah Rivka Wagner (née *Wajnert*);
born circa 1893

  Married: *Yumi Wagner*,
  no children

UNCLE (father's brother):
Chaim Moshe (haCohen) Frajlich

  Married, aunt's name unknown;
  many children, names unknown

UNCLE (father's brother):
Yechiel Mayer (haCohen) Frajlich;

  Not married; one daughter, name
  unknown, born c. 1932

*Ann Frajlich Szedlecki; born 1932
(the only member of her family to
survive the Holocaust)

  Married: *Abraham Szedlecki*

    Daughter: *Lynda Kraar*

      GRANDDAUGHTERS:
      Miriam Malka Borden
      Yona Sarah McGraw

Prologue

I am the daughter of nobody. I have no sisters. I am nobody's grand-daughter or daughter-in-law, aunt or cousin. Who am I? My past is all gone, disappeared. But I am determined to pick up the slender threads to re-establish a family tree, to reconnect the broken links and make the chain whole again.

After more than six years in the relatively safe haven of the Soviet Union, I returned to my hometown of Lodz in June 1946. Soon after my arrival I saw an announcement that the famous Jewish comedy team Dzigan and Szumacher was going to give a performance.[1] Like me, they had also fled from Lodz to the Soviet Union and had now returned home. The plainspoken Dzigan and his straight man, the intellectual Szumacher, were a perfect complement to each other. When the curtain opened on their performance, an outsized photo album stood on the stage. The two performers flanked the giant prop and when they turned each page, scenes from the lost world of pre-war Poland appeared.

Each city, town or village had its distinctive Jewish characters – beggars, fools, cripples, street vendors, water carriers and so forth,

---

1 For more on Dzigan and Szumacher, and on the other foreign names and terms used in this book, see the glossary.

and pious men calling out to the Jewish housewives, reminding them to light Shabbat candles.[2] All of these characters jumped out of the album to perform. It was an unforgettable experience, a portrait of a lost world, never to be regained. Even though they were comedians, there wasn't a dry eye in the audience. We were all very touched to see these familiar personalities who had disappeared forever from the streets of Poland, but not from our memory.

I will write as much as I can remember. Like Dzigan and Schumacher, I am opening up the pages of my life's album and reenacting it, page by page.

My parents told me a lot of stories from World War I about the Germans, the Russians, and so on. I felt that I had missed out on a lot of excitement. If only I had known what I would be missing in the near future – my entire family.

---

2 Shabbat, the Jewish Sabbath, begins at sundown on Friday night with the lighting of two candles. For more information, see the glossary.

The Curtain Rises

When I reached the bend of the road, I turned around one more time and waved a final good bye to my wonderful mother-like landlady, Katia Shkurenko. She stood on the balcony, watching me disappear, and waved back. These gestures marked my final exit from the Soviet Union and the end of this remarkable stage in my life.

I was on the road to the railway station, my luggage consisting only of what I had on my back, size twelve shoes on my feet, a bag of dry bread called *suchary*, and a jar of melted butter. I hadn't acquired much after more than six years here, but at least I was alive.

Although I came here with my older brother, Shoel, I was making the trip back alone. I left him in an unmarked grave. Three years earlier, he had succumbed to tuberculosis, the result of having been arrested, tortured during interrogation and unjustly sentenced to eight years of hard labour for a political crime he didn't commit. Shoel was only twenty-three years old when he died. I was seventeen.

Now, at the age of twenty-one, I was going back to Poland and I asked myself, for what? I didn't hold out any hope of finding that anyone from my family had survived. If they had, I would have heard from them by now. The peace was one year old, and even in these remotest areas of Russia we were quite aware of what had happened to our people.

I was going back to where my life began.

Family Portraits

No pictures exist anymore. I have to rely on my memory. Yet my family's dear faces are always in front of my eyes. Two large portraits of my mother's parents hung above their beds. My grandmother is in a high-necked blouse or dress, her wig beautifully set, adorned with drop earrings. My bearded grandfather is wearing the hat and *capote* (a long, hooded cloak) that pious men wore. Then there was a portrait of my parents taken shortly after their marriage. My father, Shimshon Frajlich, is seated and my mother, Liba Bayla Frajlich (neé Wajnert), is standing with her hand on his shoulder. She is wearing a high-necked dress and a wig.[1] My father is clean-shaven, wearing a knee-length coat.

After they got married, my parents moved to Lodz from a small town. My mother started growing her hair and my father traded in his *capote* for a suit and tie.[2] Under his hat he still wore a *kippa*, a

---

1 Married Orthodox Jewish women cover their hair when in the presence of men other than their husbands. While many do so with some form of hat or scarf, some wear a wig.

2 In some traditional circles it is also a custom for an Orthodox woman to shave her head when she marries and keep her hair short under her head covering. The fact that Ann's mother began growing her hair and her father began wearing a suit and tie after moving to the big city of Lodz represented their embrace of more modern customs.

skullcap, so that he was never bare-headed. There was a dress in my mother's wardrobe that she never wore, made of orange velvet and gold lamé, the style worn by the flappers who dared to dance the Charleston.[3] It was cut above the knee and sleeveless, I never found out where she got it, but now my guess is that it probably came from my Aunt Sarah, her youngest sister who lived in Germany and was a very well-dressed and attractive woman. The dress was beautiful – I could hardly wait to grow up and wear it.

My father was a tailor. He contracted for retail menswear stores and employed a few workers. There was a time when he was making a good living and we were comfortably well off. We could even afford a maid, Cesia, who was very devoted to us. Once the Depression arrived in Poland, my father's health began to decline and we hit hard times. We had to let Cesia go. She was willing to work just for food, but we couldn't even afford that. We no longer went to the summer cottages we used to rent or to a resort. That all became a fond memory.

Because my father was less able to provide us with our daily needs during the Depression, my mother started to help out, buying clearance merchandise and going to nearby towns and villages on market days to sell to peasants for a small profit. Sometimes I went with her. She would open a suitcase on the ground and display her merchandise. The police chased us away all the time because we had no permit. The odd time when they did manage to catch us, they confiscated everything. Somehow, we kept things going and were never hungry.

One day my poor, overworked mother asked me to go to the store for some butter. I complained that I was too tired to go. Without a word, she went to the store herself, walking down and back up the four flights of stairs to our apartment. She wasn't too tired. I remember and regret this incident every day of my life. I should have been forced to go – then I wouldn't feel guilty every time I recall it.

---

3   A popular American dance from the 1920s, considered risqué by many people at the time.

Exhausted as my mother was, I can still remember her singing. I am still puzzled by how she knew the song "A Bicycle Built for Two" in English.[4] That was the first song my granddaughters Miriam Malka and Yona Sarah learned from me, years later in Canada.

Before the war, my parents had a chance to go to America, but my mother was too afraid of boats. How different our lives would have been had they left Poland while there was still time.

My father wasn't an easy person to get to know. He was always too busy and left the raising of the children to my mother. Like many Polish Jews, Yiddish was his mother-tongue and he never learned to speak Polish fluently. A man of few words, busy from morning to night, he was the first to rise and the first to settle into bed. He never failed to put on his *tefillin* in the morning.[5] His murmured prayers still ring in my ears. He always said a blessing before he put anything in his mouth, even water. True to his faith, and despite his modern dress, he still regularly attended a *shtiebl*, a modest one-room house of prayer. I can see him after returning from Sabbath prayers, sitting at the head of our table, a head of carp on the plate in front of him. I don't remember ever getting a hug or a kiss from my father, but he never failed to take me to Simchat Torah.[6]

My mother used to say, "Your father is always immaculate. That's what attracted me to him." It was my task to take my father's detachable cuffs and collar to the laundry to get them washed and starched for the Sabbath. When it came to religious observance, my father knew that I didn't always adhere to the strict rules of the household. I followed my older siblings' secular example, but he never made an issue out of it. He never objected to the excursions I made on Saturday

---

4 A popular English song from the 1890s, also called "Daisy Bell."

5 Called phylacteries in English, *tefillin* are worn by Jews during prayer. For more information, see the glossary.

6 Simchat Torah is a festive autumn holiday that involves children and singing and dancing during the synagogue service. For more information, see the glossary.

afternoons after our Sabbath meal – to the skating rink in winter or the swimming pool in summer or to a movie.

One time I talked my father into taking me to see the musical comedy film *Jolly Fellows* that was a big hit in Poland in the 1930s – it was a Soviet film but there was no mention of communism in it that I could detect. I had seen it a few times and loved it, but, wouldn't you know it, my father fell asleep in the middle. I decided not to wake him and stayed for the second showing. There was no intermission and people were allowed to stay as long as they wanted. When my father finally woke up, he asked me, "When is the movie going to be over? I'm hungry!" He wasn't angry at me for staying, but my mother was worried, not knowing what happened to us.

In contrast to my father, my modern mother, whom I adored, loved to participate in discussions about movies and was an avid theatre and concertgoer. She got her hair done every week, spoke Polish and read both Polish and Jewish Yiddish-language newspapers. She also read the *siddur* (prayer book) and prayed with the best of them; she was also an excellent baker who came from a long line of bakers.

My older sister, Malka, a petite, green-eyed redhead whom we called Manya, was born in 1916. She excelled in school to such an extent that when she finished her last year of formally required elementary education in Grade 7, she was able to continue her education in the *gymnázium* (high school), thanks to a subsidy from the city. She was also a talented musician who played a mandolin, the neck of which was adorned with many coloured ribbons.

All of Manya's accomplishments didn't exclude her from having to help out at home – there was no free ride. She was an expert in making buttonholes by hand for the jackets that my father made. The only problem was that she was a leftist, an admirer of socialism and communism, which were illegal in Poland at that time. It was the trend amongst her friends. She quickly grew out of it, however, when she met and married Janek Ceder, a young man who owned a hardware store. Manya quickly adapted to capitalism, much to my family's relief.

My older brother, Shoel, was three years younger than Manya. He was what we called a *zibaleh*, a "preemie," who came into the world in 1919 when my mother was only seven months pregnant. He was also a redhead, but with blue eyes. Shoel wasn't a very diligent student, which we attributed to his premature birth. He developed frequent nosebleeds that were eased by following the old wives' tale of putting a bunch of keys down the back of his shirt. Strangely, the bleeding stopped, probably from the shock of having huge, heavy, cold keys come in contact with his skin.

When my father tried to introduce Shoel to tailoring, my brother said that he couldn't place the thread in the tiny eyehole of the needle because of his poor eyesight. That turned out to be just an excuse – later we found out that he had set his goals higher and found a job as a salesman in a ready-to-wear establishment, just two houses away from our home. He was a loyal son who handed over his wages to my mother, keeping very little for himself. My first pair of skates was a gift from him. At the rink, he left me in the middle so that I could take my first steps. He showed up later and when I complained, he said, "It's never too early to learn to stand on one's own feet." These would become very prophetic words that would guide me in a few years.

In 1938, just one year before the war, Shoel went to a summer resort for two weeks and I accompanied him. I stayed in a room with three other girls. At seven in the morning a maid brought us cake and milk, after which breakfast was served in the dining room. During our free time we engaged in all kinds of activities. I remember watching a very talented man built a sphinx out of sand after the rain.

I was born on June 13, 1925. They called me Chana, or usually Chanaleh, which means little Chana. My mother was thirty-eight years old and I was the youngest of five children. The oldest one and the one before me had died before I was born. They were boys. I never found out how they died and I can't even recall their names. All I can remember is that one of them had been known as a *Talmid chacham*, a gifted pupil of religious studies.

Lodz Memories

Stary Rynek No. 1

When I was born, my parents lived at Stary Rynek No. 1 – Stary Rynek means Old Market Street. We occupied one room in the attic of a tenement building. We could use only one gate to get to the tenement. On one side of the gate was a hardware store and on the other was a grocery store. Outside these stores were barrels of sour pickles, sold by the piece, as well as sauerkraut, herring and other delicacies. The hardware store sold kerosene to light the lamps. There was electricity, but not everyone could afford it. Every time I smell kerosene or bite into a sour pickle, nostalgia overcomes me, and I go back to the place of my early childhood.

The tenement had three wooden balconies that encircled every floor and in the middle of the courtyard was a well for water. The huge wheel had to be turned to bring water to the surface. We weren't connected to the city's water system, so we had an outhouse in place of a toilet.

One of my earliest memories is of the day one of our neighbours held a wedding with many guests on the balcony. The young couple was under the *chuppah*, the wedding canopy, when the balcony collapsed under their weight. The newlyweds fell on the wheel of the

well, which was turning at the time. They were the only fatalities of
this tragic accident.

Polnocna No. 7

When I was about five years old, we moved to a ground floor flat at
Polnocna No. 7 – Polnocna means North Street. Our financial situation had improved, and now our living quarters consisted of two
rooms and a kitchen. Half of the kitchen was my mother's domain
and the other half was my father's – he had turned it into a work area
for his tailoring. There were four sewing machines and one bench for
a presser who used a charcoal iron, a large table for my father to prepare bundles for operators and a table for the garment finishers.

Our dining room consisted of a beautiful dining table set with six
black chairs with brown leather seats. Instead of legs, the table had
a storage space where we kept our Passover dishes.[1] Above the table
was a beautiful crystal chandelier, that sparkled and gave off magnificent rainbows of colour when it was switched on. We had a huge
credenza, filled with all kinds of knickknacks. The chandelier caused
us a lot of concern, especially at Simchat Torah, which is a very joyous
holiday. The part-owner of this complex and his family lived above
our flat. They were very religious and had many guests during the
holidays. They danced for hours and hours, and the fixture would
sway ominously back and forth.

My sister slept on the couch and my brother on a folding bed in
the dining room. I still slept in my baby bed in my parents' bedroom
– in fact I slept in that bed for many years until I was much too big for
it. My parents slept in twin beds that were next to each other and cov-

---

1 During the Jewish festival of Passover, which takes place over eight days in the
spring, observant Jews follow a set of specific dietary restrictions and often use
a separate set of dishes that are used only at this time of the year. For more on
Passover and the observances associated with it, see the glossary.

ered with a heavy, burgundy velour bedspread. We kept our clothes in a huge wardrobe that also had drawers for linens since we had no built-in closets.

Our improved financial situation didn't last long – soon after we moved into Polnocna No. 7 we began experiencing hard times due to the Depression. One piece of our dining room set, the credenza, was taken by the city for non-payment of taxes. No sooner did we ransom it than another piece was taken for the same reason until it too was redeemed. But we were hit the hardest when the city officials took the wardrobe. Hooks went up the walls to hang our clothes and other things were kept on the floor. We had to do the same thing when we later moved to a much smaller place with only one room and a kitchen. We never got our beautiful dining room set back, but by then we had no room for it anyway.

As I mentioned earlier, my father did contracting for large retail stores. Even though he often had trouble collecting the money they owed him, the workers still had to be paid, so many times we had to dig into our own meagre resources to pay them. One winter things got so bad that my mother had to start a soup kitchen to serve people working outdoors to help us through the tough times.

Later, as the Depression took its toll on us, my father had to charge less money for his garments in order to keep working and he had to cut his workers' wages. This caused a lot of strife and ill feelings between the employers and the employees, and strikes by garment workers became quite common. Since my father had to deliver finished goods to the stores on time or risk losing the contracts, he had to hire strikebreakers. Feelings about this ran so high that my father was actually knifed one day.

My father was a *cohen*, meaning that he belonged to a revered group of Jewish men considered to be descendants of the high priests of the Bible-era Temple. The designation carries certain religious restrictions, including the restriction that a *cohen* cannot come near a dead body. When a resident of our tenement passed away, his body was kept at home until the day of the burial because there were no funeral homes. On the day that my father was knifed, a body was being kept very near to the outhouse so my father couldn't use it. Instead, he had to use the one in the next house and he was attacked on his way back home. When my mother tried to catch the perpetrators by jumping out the window of our ground-floor flat, she fell and twisted her ankle. Both my parents had to be taken to the hospital, but their injuries weren't serious and they were released after being examined.

It turned out that one of our relatives, who was also one of my father's striking employees, was the instigator but had paid someone else to carry out the attack. No charges were laid, because nobody was killed

To make matters worse, my father wasn't a very healthy man and frequently came down with pneumonia. He kept his cough medicine, which consisted of valerian drops with mint, in the medicine cabinet that was part of the wall clock. He wound that clock every morning with a key that he kept in the breast pocket of his vest. Whenever his cough was bad, he put a few drops of this remedy on a cube of sugar and sucked on it. We never used saccharine because my father claimed that it weakened the heart. This resonated with me so much that to this day I have never used an artificial sweetener. My father was also convinced that he only had dreams when his stomach was upset. On those days, he ate nothing but bread with onions or radishes.

My parents owned the apartment that we lived in at Polnocna No. 7. They had bought it from an elderly Orthodox couple who lived above us. When the couple passed away, however, their daughter and her family moved in and the troubles began. They tried to force us to pay rent by threatening to throw us out. I couldn't understand how they could do it unless the ownership agreement with her parents had only been a verbal one. They even brought in police and accused us of stealing when their apartment was turned upside down. But the police established that they had done it themselves.

After many court appearances, nothing was resolved and my parents decided to throw in the towel. The final case took place in early March 1935 during a particularly bad snowstorm. I don't know what the verdict was, but a few months later, we loaded our possessions onto a horse-drawn platform and moved into one room and a kitchen in a poorer neighbourhood that would later become part of the Lodz ghetto.

All this trouble was caused by God-fearing people who took their Jewishness very seriously, but had little regard for people. Unfortunately, Hitler would soon make us all equal.

Public School No. 132 for Jewish Girls

When I turned seven, I started my education at Public School No. 132. The school – for Jewish girls only – was located on the third floor of an apartment building. It was very near to where we lived and my sister took me there sometimes, but most of the time I went alone. It was very crowded – there were sixty of us in a class with four pupils to a desk and there was no playground. I was in awe of the principal, Pani (Mrs.) Borzykowski, and was afraid to enter her private office. I guess that her title scared me.

A year later the school relocated to a brand new building on Wierzbowa, Willow Street, an amazing, modern building with parquet floors and a fully equipped gym. The gym also had a stage and on it was a piano that our music teacher used to accompany us when we practiced for the choir. As in the smaller facility, the classrooms each held sixty pupils. Even though these new classrooms were roomy with big windows, they were still quite crowded, still with four to a desk. The desks had built-in inkwells and we had to dip our pens in the ink to write – there were no such things as ballpoint pens.

White-aproned workers dispensed meals from the well-equipped kitchen. Boiled milk was free and the meals were free for those who couldn't afford to pay. My favourite lunch was a sandwich of sprats, eggs and a slice of dill pickle. The school banned onions because of the smell. We all wore slippers at school. Our shoes and boots in the winter were left in a cloakroom in the basement along with the coats – there weren't any lockers. Half of the yard was paved and during recess, we played games – mostly what we called football – on it. The other half was used to grow vegetables. They were planted in the spring and were ripe by the time we got back to school for a new academic term. Unfortunately, the students weren't able to gather the last crop in 1939.

From Grade 1 to Grade 3, our teacher was a Polish Catholic lady named Janina Szmoniewska and we adored her. Classes were taught in Polish and she taught us all subjects. She was very fair. I remember going on a school trip to a museum where we saw the liver of an alcoholic preserved in a jar. We also visited a brewery and a school for the blind. Once a month we went to the movies. For every ten paid admissions, one was free and went to a pupil who couldn't afford to pay. This was done very democratically and we never found out who the recipient was, but I never was one of them. The school also had another tradition: before Rosh Hashanah, the Jewish New Year, and Passover we were asked to bring in food items to be distributed among needy students. We never knew who was being helped, all I knew was that I was the giver. This tradition was instilled in me from an early age.

From Grade 4 on we had different teachers for each subject, although we stayed in the same classroom. The teacher I liked least was Miss Epstajn, a spinster who had a chronic respiratory condition. She taught arithmetic, which, by the way, I hated. I eventually learned to love working with figures when I worked as a bookkeeper and, later, when I became the proprietor of Albion Style Shoppe, a retail dress shop in Toronto.

We sometimes played tricks on Miss Epstajn, especially on April Fools' Day, which we called Prima Aprilis. One year she came into the classroom only to discover that nobody was there – we had all gone to the park. She was a good sport about it, though, and we weren't punished.

The unsightly and very strict Mrs. Rajchman taught us Polish, geography, history and other subjects, and she demanded courtesy from us. When we met her in the hallway of the school, she expected us to carry her books. When she took us on field trips, she always warned us not to behave like Jewish *bachory*, brats. We resented that very much because, after all, she was also Jewish. Our gentile teachers never called us that.

I loved to listen to stories from the Bible that our religion teacher read to us. Our state-run public school required us to have two hours of religious instruction every day. I don't know what people in Western countries would make of that today.

To say that we were Polish patriots is not an exaggeration – we were proud to wave the red-and-white Polish flag. We took part in several parades, carrying our school colours. When Marshal Józef Piłsudski died on May 12, 1935, the whole country – particularly the Jewish community – was in mourning.[2] He had been a very popular war hero and Jews worried that things might get tougher after his death. As it turned out, some of these suspicions were justified. We wore black armbands for a whole month as a sign of mourning and respect. Our school attended a memorial in the magnificent Great Synagogue, which was also known as the Reform or Deutsche Shul.[3]

Constitution Day, May 3, was a national holiday that marked the signing of the first Polish constitution in 1791 and our school participated in the parade. I remember that one year, I was assigned to take

---

2 Marshal Józef Piłsudski led the independent Second Polish Republic from 1918 to 1935. He was viewed positively by the Polish Jewish community because they felt he was able to keep antisemitic currents in check. For more information, see the glossary.

3 Opened in 1887, the Great Synagogue of Lodz was the most modern and progressive Jewish institution in the city. Considered one of the most beautiful in all of Europe, it was also a venue for concerts and the celebration of national holidays and events – such as the memorial service for Piłsudski. For more information, see the glossary. Shul is the Yiddish word for synagogue.

the school's flag to the principal's office when we returned. I stood glued to the floor, petrified to enter her inner sanctum, until someone finally took the flag from me, to my great relief.

Our classes started at eight o'clock in the morning and continued until two in the afternoon. My mother gave me forty-five groszy for a return streetcar ride, but I preferred to run and save the money for the movies.[4] I took the "scenic" route home, past beautiful Stasnica Park with its centuries-old trees and then on toward Helenów Park with its swimming pool in the summer and skating rink in the winter. I went past the huge Poznanski hospital, endowed by the late Jewish businessman Izrael K. Poznanski. He was famous for being a successful Jewish manufacturer of fabrics in Lodz at the end of the nineteenth century. I also ran past the Jewish home for the aged. When I finally got home, we all had our main meal and then I was ready to do my homework. Sometimes I had to pull basting from garments for my father. Most of the time, though, my mother released me from this task.

I didn't make too many friends at school, but I remember a few girls fondly. One of them was Fela Radomska, with her beautiful black eyes. She was a very good student who lived in the good part of Lodz. Her family had a piano in their salon and they spoke Polish amongst themselves. Hela Aronowicz was an excellent student whose beautiful penmanship I envied. Tall, good-looking Lewkowicz was a curly redhead with one blue eye and one brown eye. I couldn't stop staring at her, but she was used to it. I remember Bronia and also beautiful, curly-haired Tymianko, whom I used to study with. Fela Domb was another beauty whose lovely smile lit up the room. I met Fela's older sister after the war and she told me that the rest of the family had survived Auschwitz only to be killed by the Allies when they bombed the train on which they were being taken to Germany. What an irony, to have survived the enemy only to be killed by friendly fire.

---

4 Groszy are Polish currency coins of low monetary value like pennies.

Our Neighbourhood

In 1935 we moved again to Podrzeczna No. 12. The street name means Under-the-River Street, although there was no visible river in the city as it was underground. Podrzeczna was commonly referred to as *der yiddisher gasse*, the Jewish street; it would later become part of the Lodz ghetto. The Jewish area of Lodz began at Plac Wolności, Freedom Square, from which four streets branched out. In the middle of the square stood a statue of Tadeusz Kosciusko, the Polish military hero who took part in the American War of Independence.[5] In another corner was the city hall, with its large clock on the roof. Polish women sold flowers in the square when the weather turned warm; you could weigh yourself on a public scale for five groszy. All around the square retail stores sold a variety of goods and a huge billboard featured the Dionne quintuplets endorsing Palmolive products.[6]

Our neighbourhood was full of smells – good and bad. The stench could be horrible as the butcher and fish shop smells mingled with the unpleasant odours from the tannery where sheepskin was processed. On the second floor in the corner apartment of the tenement we lived in was a small outfit that manufactured sandals with soles made of *kauchuk*, Indian rubber. I liked the smell of it. You could call me a glue sniffer, but of course there was no such word in our vocabulary at the time.

If you took a few steps down from the corner, though, you would be greeted by the most wonderful aromas from the bakery. My favou-

---

5 Tadeusz Kosciuszko was a hero in Poland because, in addition to his military exploits in the North America, he had also led a failed uprising to oust Russian occupiers from Poland in 1794, after which the country ceased to exist until 1918.

6 The Dionne quintuplets, born in Canada in 1934, were the first quintuplets known to survive infancy and the only female identical set ever recorded. They were extremely popular in the 1930s and 1940s and, throughout their childhood, they were used as an attraction and for marketing purposes around the world.

rite of their famous breads was the pumpernickel with raisins. Their other baked goods such as pastries, challahs and cookies attracted customers from other parts of the city.

Across from the bakery, a tiny store sold cosmetics. If you wanted perfume by the gram, you had to bring your own vial. This store also had the only phone on the street. You could use it for ten groszy, which I did when I had to call my brother-in-law at his hardware store. Wonderful spicy smells also wafted from Dishkin's Deli. Their goose salamis, cold cuts, liver pâté and hot dogs were famous. With each purchase we got a free serving of mustard so strong that it watered your eyes and cleared your sinuses.

Across the street was a well-stocked liquor store. If you think that Jews are not alcoholic-beverage swillers, think again. The store was always busy, especially before holidays – with the exception of Passover, when many housewives, including my mother, made their own wine. Some people brewed their own beer and kept the barrels on balconies. We kids were allowed to drink wine as part of the Sabbath ritual blessing.[7]

There was also a *schenk*, or pub – the closest translation would be a licensed delicatessen – where delicious local fare was served. My favourites were *kishke* and *miltz* – the intestine of a cow, stuffed with flour, fat and spices, and cow's lung. There were more traditional foods such as chicken soup with noodles or with kreplach, dumplings stuffed with meat. Some people came in just to socialize and have a stein of beer and a pretzel. The *schenk* did big business in take-out. Sometimes we were sent there to bring home food for our evening meal, mostly in the winter when we felt like having something hot. I particularly liked *vemplech*, tripe – the velvety second stomach lining of a cow or ox – that was spicy and cheap. Strangely enough, the

7 The two main meals of Shabbat, on Friday night and Saturday afternoon, begin with a blessing over a cup of wine, called kiddush.

schenk was called *Der Bridige Shmuel*, Dirty Samuel. Despite its moniker, though, it was spotless.

Hand-churned vanilla ice cream was sold from a little kiosk. A cone was five groszy; for ten groszy a much larger portion of ice cream was put between shell-shaped edible wafers. In what looked like a hallway, Fat Zlata sat behind the counter in her apron, selling soda water by the bottle – your own – or the glass. If you wanted it sweet, she added syrup, at an extra cost. My favourite flavour was *limonada* (lemonade). After someone used the glass, it was rinsed in a basin, not under running water. I don't know how often she changed the water in the basin, but we never caught any germs.

The street vendors selling hot dogs, pretzels or bagels were a shabby, dirty lot who sold their wares from baskets displayed on the ground. These poor souls, mainly street people, didn't have permits and were constantly being chased by police. In the pursuit they would lose their livelihood until they were able to replenish their stock by whatever means.

There was a hand laundry, always full of steam. This was where I took the detachable cuffs and collars of my father's shirts every week to be washed and starched stiff as a board for him to wear to synagogue on Saturdays. My father would also send me to the corner kiosk to buy Grand Prix cigarettes every morning before I went to school. I was allowed to buy cigarettes since there were no laws at that time forbidding the sale of tobacco to minors. These kiosks were run by World War I veterans or disabled people; this is how they supported themselves and maintained a sense of dignity. Poles are known for their pride – if only they'd used it in positive ways. My father lit a cigarette after each meal, took a few puffs, extinguished it, and then put the cigarette into the pack and the pack back in his vest pocket until next time.

My mother's middle sister, Tauba Glika, lived just down the street from us at Podrzeczna No. 3. She was married to Hersh Wagner, who had a little hole-in-the-wall shop that sold men's ready-to-wear. It was legitimate – he had a permit and paid taxes to the city. Where our apartment had a window facing a courtyard, Aunt Tauba had a balcony that faced the street and from this observation point I used to watch people going about their business.

Next to us, at No. 10 Podrzeczna, was a mikvah,[8] a ritual bath, and a *shtiebl*, a small one-room synagogue. No fancy synagogues for us plain folk. The oven that heated the water for the bathhouse also served as the communal oven. On Fridays, my mother and other housewives would bring their *cholent*, traditional stew, and cakes and challahs there; after simmering overnight, we would pick up the *cholent* on Saturday at noon for the midday meal. We ate ours after my father came back from the *shtiebl*.[9]

Some of our relatives lived on the other side of us at Podrzeczna No. 14. I remember a commotion when one of the girls who lived there was about to get married. On the day of the wedding the groom refused to show up until he got the promised dowry. A car was dispatched to get him while the guests waited. He got his money and the wedding went on as planned.

A Day In the Life of Podrzeczna No. 12

In our own tenement, Podrzeczna No. 12, we all slept in one room and the kitchen again served two purposes – as my father's much-reduced work area and my mother's kitchen. It was here that I was

---

8 A mikvah is the ritual purification bath taken by observant Jews on certain occasions; the word also refers to the building that houses the bath. For more information, see the glossary

9 Many Jewish communities in Eastern Europe had communal ovens to assist Jews cooking for Shabbat and to make it possible to serve a hot meal on Saturday afternoons. For more information, see the glossary. A challah is the special braided egg bread that is traditionally served on Shabbat. *Cholent* is a traditional slow-cooked meat, bean and vegetable stew.

allowed to have a dog for the first time. It was a little black mutt with brown paws and a brown-tipped nose. I loved it and I endowed it with a great name: Lord. We were actually considered quite well off – many families larger than ours were crowded into one room and a kitchen. There was no running water or indoor plumbing. We had a key to the outhouse, which was kept clean by a janitor. In order to bathe, we used water from the well in the courtyard. The janitor, the only gentile in our tenement, had to activate the motor to bring the water to the surface to fill up our pails. Once we had water it had to be heated and put into a basin – we washed our hair first and then stepped into the basin to finish bathing. If you missed getting water from the janitor, you had to wait till the next day or get a water carrier to supply you with some – for a charge, of course. Our water carrier was a young, mildly retarded man named Beniek who was always serenading the girls. In the first days of the Nazi occupation he was killed by a soldier for pointing a finger at him. He was lucky that at least he didn't end up in a death camp.

In front of the building there was one entrance for pedestrians, another for the horse-and-buggy traffic that delivered or took out goods all day. The wooden staircase inside the building was very narrow. A man named Sherman who lived on the floor above us was often stricken with an asthma attack and it was a real problem for the ambulance attendants to carry the stretcher down.

Each window of Podrezna No. 12 looked out onto the courtyard and the view was our contact with the outside world and our source of news and information. From the window I'd watch my mother with a wicker basket on her arm going out to do early shopping for our daily supplies since we had no refrigerator. I'd wait for her to come back and make breakfast for us. I often sat by the window and observed the daily rituals of our neighbours and friends.

About 150 families shared this courtyard, so there were a lot of family and community functions. There were happy ones such as weddings, engagement parties, bar mitzvahs and birth celebrations.

Bat mitzvahs were unheard of back then.[10] I often went to these gatherings, mainly to collect the candies thrown by guests, which was a tradition on these happy occasions. When a poor or orphaned girl got engaged, we all helped her start her own household with whatever we could spare – a pot, a pan, linens or other items. This was our version of a bridal shower. There were also sombre occasions. Dead bodies were kept in the home until the funeral, and the processions came through the courtyard. The little *shtiebl* beside us served everybody.

The daily activities started early. From our courtyard we could see groups of people rushing to begin work at seven in the morning. They were tailors, shoemakers, furriers, weavers, dressmakers and others. Employers like my father had to be up early to prepare the bundles so that the workers wouldn't waste any time. School began at eight o'clock and a parade of children of all ages headed out to make their class on time. The younger ones carried backpacks while the older ones carried attaché cases. Everyone had a lunch box.

Peasant women came into the courtyard in the morning carrying huge milk containers and measuring cups, and housewives lined up to buy from them. There was no pasteurization, so the milk had to be boiled. These women came on milk trains from outlying villages and they had to be up very early to milk the cows and catch the train.

The owner of the hardware store located in front of our building used the other apartment on our floor to store merchandise. Large items too big to steal, like corrugated sheets of metal, were left outside in the courtyard leaning against the wall. I remember hearing a strange sound one day, like water running over the metal sheets. It was a man urinating on the merchandise! If that wasn't enough, people from the upper floors emptied their chamber pots out the

---

10 A bar mitzvah is the Jewish ritual and family celebration that marks the religious coming of age of a boy at the age of thirteen. In the latter half of the twentieth century, liberal Jews began the practice of a bat mitzvah – a similar ceremony for a girl that takes place at the age of twelve. For more information, see the glossary.

window, sometimes on an unsuspecting person below. It was either that or carry the pots all the way to the outhouse at the end of the courtyard. It was safer to walk in the middle of the courtyard and many people did.

Throughout the day we heard the sound of foot-operated sewing machines – there were no electric ones. The pressers sprayed water from their mouths onto the fabric to make it easier to press. We could also hear the sounds of shoemakers hammering as they repaired shoes and see the steam rising from the laundry as the housewives boiled the clothes in huge vats before the actual wash. We were lucky to be able to hire a woman to do our laundry at her home. She would return it, ironed and fresh smelling.

Everything came to a standstill on Fridays and all day Saturday for Shabbat. Sundays, though, were a different matter. I went to school on Sunday, but by law we weren't allowed to work on that day. Unfortunately, we couldn't afford to have two days off – nobody could. The working season, particularly for tailors, was very short. So a plan was devised to enable us to work on Sunday and have that extra piece of meat on the plate.

Each Sunday somebody would stand guard at the gate of the tenement to alert us if they saw the police approaching. As soon as they were spotted, the look-out would call out, "Zeks!" I never found out what this meant, although it is the Yiddish word for the number six. Immediately, the sewing machines would be covered and the workers would sit down to play cards. It was a cat-and-mouse game – the police knew what was going on. Many of them were corrupt and left quietly after taking a *łapówka*, a bribe. They also needed that extra income and were happy to look the other way.

During the summer everyone kept their windows open. Sometimes a group of acrobats would come to the courtyard, spread a carpet on the ground and put on a show with somersaults, pyramids and jumps. Watching them gave the women a respite from their chores and a change from their routine, if only for a short while. They wrapped small coins, whatever they could spare, in bits of paper and threw them out the window, where they were promptly collected by the entertainers.

When the acrobats made their exit, another troupe – this time musicians – would sometimes appear in a procession of men playing instruments, mostly violins, and women singing. The women's heads were covered with colourful kerchiefs like a scene from Molly Picon's movie, *Yidl mitn Fidl* (Yidl with His Fiddle).[11] Their songs were sad, mostly about unhappy love affairs and the woes of life. They were also rewarded with some coins.

Next up, a man carrying a burlap bag would amble along plaintively calling out, "Alteh schmattes!" (Old rags!") The rags he managed to buy would be sold for recycling. Another man sometimes came to buy up potato peels to sell to farmers for livestock feed. How these men made a living is hard to imagine. Life was incredibly difficult and there wasn't much waste.

Between two and three in the afternoon families would take a break to have lunch, which was the main meal of the day and was eaten with all the family together. After lunch, the second part of the day's entertainment would begin with a stream of paupers – blind ones, lame ones and people with a multitude of other afflictions led by small children for added effect. They asked for food, knowing the exact time of day to appear when there might be leftovers. The official Beggars' Day was Thursday and my mother had a special cup filled with groszy for that purpose. We didn't even bother closing the door on that day – the stream was endless. I remember one beggar in particular who was called Maurice the *yekke*, a slang term for German Jews who were so proper that they wore jackets even on the hottest days. He had been an excellent ladies' custom tailor in Germany until

---

11 The 1936 film *Yidl mitn Fidl* was the most successful Yiddish-language film of all time. New York-born Molly Picon was an icon in Yiddish-language entertainment circles. For more information, see the glossary.

he lost his mind and wound up back in Poland years before the war. He slept on the staircase of Podrzeczna No. 7 and lived on handouts; how he survived winters I do not know.

I have a confession to make: more than once I sinned for the love of ice cream. Once I helped myself to five groszy from my mother's special alms cup to treat myself to an ice cream. I still feel guilty every time I eat ice cream and never pass a panhandler without putting a few coins in his cup. Another time, my love for ice cream almost desecrated our strictly kosher household.[12] One of our employees took me aside one day and said, "Can you bring me a kaiser bun with ham? I'll give you money for ice cream if you do it." I walked to the *tref* (non-kosher) delicatessen and hesitated, passing in front many times. Inside I looked around – it was spotless. When I placed the order, I felt like a traitor. They looked at me curiously but didn't say anything. I guess many Jews patronized their store. When I came home, my father asked me to put the brown bag on the table, picked it up with his scissors – he wouldn't dare touch it with his hands – and threw it out. And I thought he hadn't noticed the transaction! "If you wanted a *nosh* (snack), you should have asked me," my father sternly told me. But I wasn't punished for my crime.

In summer, our evening meals consisted of my favourite dark bread with raisins, Swiss cheese and a hot drink, usually coffee or tea. For a cheaper blend, we substituted chicory for the coffee beans.

Things started slowing down around seven in the evening. Exhausted workers went home to their own families after a hard day. The employers, including my father, still had to get things ready for the next day. After that, hardships forgotten, people got dressed up for a date, to go dancing, to see a movie, or to just go for a walk along

---

12 Observant Jews follow a system of rules about what to eat, how to prepare food and how meat and poultry are slaughtered (known as *kashruth* or keeping kosher.) Among other things, the consumption of pork products is forbidden. For more information, see the glossary.

Pietrokovska Street, the main drag. It was lined with brightly lit ice cream parlours and cafés stocked with delicious pastries where you could sit as long as you wanted, surrounded by friends, carrying on discussions – mostly about politics in those days, groups of people trying to improve the world. You were never pressured to give up your table.

Each tenement gate was closed at eleven at night. If you arrived home later than that, you had to call the janitor by pulling a wire connected to a bell in his quarters. He didn't mind, even if it meant being awoken several times during the night. The tips he collected supplemented his meagre income. By that time the courtyard was quiet, except in the summer, when a few people sat outside cooling off or maybe having another cigarette. One more day of sights, sounds and smells came to an end. Tomorrow the cycle would begin again.

Growing Up

From the youngest age I was exposed to a house full of young people, mostly friends of my older siblings. They engaged in conversations, political arguments, how to make the world a better place and the stuff of young life. All that was needed was a hand-cranked *gramafon* (record player), a case of beer and some pretzels, and the party was on. I learned to dance the Charleston before I learned the alphabet.

In the winter I went ice skating and got pretty good at it. In the summer months I went to the public swimming pool. The only way to get to the pool was to take the streetcar loop in Lodz and then change from city cars to the ones that went out of town. The pool was in a gentile area and most Jews avoided it, but I don't recall any trouble there. A certain part of Spadina Avenue in Toronto reminds me of that streetcar loop. When we got off the streetcar, we had to walk to reach the pool. I loved to walk among the tall stalks of wheat and patches of potatoes along the way.

One day I went to the pool with my sister wearing only a pair of green pants with suspenders and no shirt underneath. After all, I was only ten years old, with only my flat chest exposed. When I got into the pool, I found a rubber, balloon-like object, filled it with water and ran back to show my sister, who was with her friends. The group gaped in shock at my new plaything and blushed with embarrassment. I had no idea what the fuss was all about. It took me a few years to realize that it was a condom, although I already knew the facts of life. I knew why my sister needed sanitary napkins. Sometimes I was sent to the *apteka*, the pharmacy, to get them. One time my father caught me reading my sister's book about sex. He just took it out of my hands without fuss or comment.

In the summer we attended concerts in Helenów Park, which also had a small zoo. The most popular animal was an ape we called in Yiddish "Yanek mitn Roiteh Tuches" – Yanek with the Red Ass. The park had tall bushes that hid a lovers' lane and an artificial lake where you could rent a rowboat. I used to sit on the edge and watch tadpoles; when I'd come back the next time, they were already frogs.

There was also a band shell where, as soon as the weather turned warm, wonderful concerts were held. A very popular quartet named Choir Dana sang the latest hits there. I remember a funny story I heard about them. They had been invited to perform in the Soviet Union and when they got to the border they were asked what they had to declare. They answered that they were bringing in some *pushki* – in Polish, that means tin cans, but in Russian it means cannons! I learned the song "Tiger Rag" from listening to them. After the war we never heard from them again and I have wondered whether they were Jewish.

Even now, I only have to close my eyes when I listen to music from that era and I could swear that I hear the whispering of the tall trees, probably centuries old, accompanying it, the sweetest sound from my happy childhood. Music very often brings tears to my eyes. It always connects me to my life with my family, as brief as that was.

Not all my memories of life before the war are good ones, though. We had our share of deviants and predators in our cozy little neighbourhood and I had several encounters that I never reported to my mother, although I should have.

One of them occurred in the outhouse in our tenement on Polnocna Street. The outhouse was actually connected by a thin wall to another one that belonged to another building on the adjoining street and the wall had a hole in it. I was using it one day and heard a man's voice asking me to come closer to the peep hole. When I approached, he asked me to touch something. To my horror, it was his penis. Frightened, I ran away as fast as my legs would carry me. For the longest time afterward I was afraid to go to the outhouse alone and developed a severe case of constipation.

Another incident that caused me great discomfort involved a visit from one of our relatives. I'm no longer sure what happened, but it made me run to my mother and hide my face. Was it something he did to me? I don't remember – I've blocked it out of my mind. What I do remember about this particular visit is that we weren't invited to his wedding and he bragged about what a great affair it had been, only attended by members of the upper class. It didn't take long for my brother to reply, "If we had known, we would have sent our own Lord," invoking the name of our dog. We all burst out laughing and I don't recall another visit from this relative.

I was also once approached by a young man when my mother sent me to the store to buy dill pickles. He asked me to deliver a note to his girlfriend on the second floor, promising me ten groszy – enough for a large ice cream. I became suspicious when he started stalling and closing in on me. Fortunately, I heard some voices coming up the stairs and I escaped. "I lost the money," I told my mother when I returned home late and empty-handed. "That's why I was late coming back," I pleaded. "I was trying to find the money!"

A few years later, after we moved to Podrzeczna Street, I saw a man watching me and masturbating. At the time, I didn't understand what he was doing, but it terrified me and I couldn't move. I guess you can't go through life without being exposed to events like these. I'm not sure what the effect of them was and what has made me remember these things and write them down now. It's somehow connected – as if we were all in the jaws of something terrible and didn't know it. The times we were living in brought out the worst – not only in bad people, but in good ones as well.

In addition to doing contract work, my father began manufacturing and selling men's jackets, which was his specialty, to supplement our income. He wasn't very successful at it and eventually had to give it up. One of our customers came from Toruń, a city northwest of Lodz, to pick up the merchandise he had preordered to take to his ready-to-wear store. When he invited my sister to have supper with him, my parents gave their permission. After all, he was a family man, religious, and well-to-do, so what harm could there be? Besides, we didn't want to antagonize him – we needed the extra income. My sister came back early and told us that he had ordered room service at the hotel. He tried to give her a diamond ring in exchange for sex. She had politely refused and left. He never came back for his merchandise, but we shipped it out to him. After all, he had paid for it. Even though we lost that extra source of income, my sister kept her virginity.

There would later be times when I could have exchanged my virginity if not for a diamond ring then for a piece of bread or a meal. My sister set a good example for me, however. I kept her standard.

More Family Portraits

Kalmen Frajlich

Every year I eagerly anticipated one visit in particular – that of Kalmen Frajlich, my grandfather on my father's side. My other grandparents had all died before I was born. Every January he came for a month from Lowicz where he lived with his second wife. For some strange reason he had taken her surname – Fajbusiak – when they married. Kalmen Frajlich was a tall man with a snow-white beard that reached almost to his waist. I remember that he carried a small bottle of liquor in one of his pockets and he would reach for it from time to time. I don't remember where he slept when he visited. There were five of us, but somehow, we managed. One summer my parents sent me to spend some time with him and his new family. His wife didn't look favourably upon my presence. As a matter of fact, they didn't attend my sister's wedding – the wedding of his first granddaughter. Maybe she was jealous because her own daughter never married.

My grandfather was a tailor during the week – except on Fridays, when he became the keeper of the large community oven. I fondly remember the letters that I received from Kalmen Frajlich, written in Polish in green ink. It was very rare that someone his age would be able to write in this language.

There is a saying in Yiddish that I didn't understand as a child, "Ich hob dich in Lowicz"; loosely translated it means, "I hope you wind up in Lowicz." I only learned many decades later that Lowicz had one of the largest Jewish cemeteries in Poland.

Aunt Sarah and Uncle Yumi

My mother's youngest sister, Sarah Rivka (née Wajnert), and her husband, Benjamin Wagner, who was known as Yumi, decided to leave Lodz after World War I to live in Berlin. There they established Wagner's, a ready-to-wear retail business at Spitlemarkt Strasse No 14. Many of their store windows carried signs such as "WAGNER IS DOCH BILLIG" (WAGNER'S IS CHEAPER).

Uncle Yumi bought an automobile and was unfortunately involved in an accident that killed a German woman. I was too young to have been told all the details, but I do remember that certain conditions were put on him that would have made it impossible to re-enter Germany if he returned to Poland and neither of them ever became German citizens. Aunt Sarah was allowed to come and go across the border into Poland as she pleased and their financial situation enabled both of them to travel all over Europe, especially to health spas. They didn't consider Yumi's travel restrictions to be much of a hardship. After all, what did Poland have to offer after only a few years of independence?[1] Besides, they were proud of their newly acquired German sophistication.

Aunt Sarah came to Lodz quite often, for the *yahrzeit* of her parents, or just to visit the rest of the family.[2] Being childless, she doted

---

1 Poland was proclaimed an independent state at the end of World War I and remained so until the outbreak of World War II in September 1939. For more than a century prior to World War I, Poland was partitioned and ruled by Austria, Prussia and Russia.

2 *Yahrzeit* is the commemoration of the anniversary of a Jewish person's death by the child, spouse, sibling or parent of the deceased.

on the three of us kids. Whenever Aunt Sarah came to visit I was fascinated with the gold toothpick she used to clean her gold-capped teeth. Sometimes my mother met her in the Free City of Danzig/ Gdańsk and sometimes my mother visited Sarah and Yumi in Berlin.[3]

In our photo album we had a picture of a man in a tuxedo holding a banjo. His name was Morris Warshovsky and Sarah had once been engaged to him. She broke off the engagement because he was migrating to America and she didn't want to leave her family in Poland. Instead she married Yumi Wagner and it so happened that my mother's middle sister, Aunt Tauba, married Herschel Wagner, Uncle Yumi's brother. So the two Wajnert sisters were married to two Wagner brothers.

Sometime around 1931, when I wasn't yet six years old, my mother decided to take me with her to Berlin to visit Aunt Sarah and Uncle Yumi. We had our passport pictures taken, and I remember having to stand on a stool to be level with her. We travelled by train and during one transfer the belt of our suitcase broke; if it hadn't been for a kind stranger, we would have missed our connection.

Since Uncle Yumi wasn't allowed to drive anymore, their chauffeur met us in Berlin. Aunt Sarah and Uncle Yumi lived above their business in an apartment that could be reached either by a separate entrance or a spiral iron staircase inside the store. Their bedroom was full of throw cushions and the dining room had a beautiful crystal chandelier that sparkled. The maid was called by pulling a cord attached to the fixture. She would appear wearing a white apron, her head covered with a lace scarf, and ask, "What does *gnädige Frau* (madam) wish?"

I'm not sure how long our visit lasted, but I do remember going to the amusement park with its many rides. We also visited Kaiser

---

3 Danzig/ Gdańsk is a city state and seaport on the Baltic Sea, located about 340 kilometres from Lodz and 500 kilometres from Berlin. It belonged to Germany prior to World War I but was made an autonomous "Free City" by the peace settlement following it. For more information, see the glossary.

Willhelm Castle, where we had to put a pair of felt slippers on over our shoes so as not to mar the beautiful parquet floors. We went shopping in Tietz Department Store, where I stared in fascination at the escalator but was too terrified to ride it. My aunt bought me my very first doll on that trip. When we returned to Lodz, though, the doll somehow lost an arm. We never repaired it and it sat on my bed with its one arm. Every morning during my visit my aunt gave me a few pfennig to buy ice cream.[4] I couldn't speak German, so I asked for a *loda*, which was Yiddish and Polish for ice cream, but the people in the shop always understood what I wanted. One morning the storekeeper followed me home to see who I was. From that day on, she gave me a sucker for free whenever I visited her store.

One night we were awakened by the sound of breaking glass and ran downstairs to find the cause of the noise. The store's windows had been shattered by rocks and there was glass everywhere, but because there were no witnesses, the police couldn't – or wouldn't – do anything about it. Although the signs of trouble ahead were beginning to show, the Jews in Germany chose to ignore them. Surely, in a civilized country like Germany the Jews were quite safe, they reasoned, these were just isolated incidents. History would soon prove how wrong they were.

When all of this happened, I was just a preschooler, not yet six years old, but for me, it was my personal Kristallnacht.[5] Through the years it has remained forever etched in my memory. My aunt and uncle's Kristallnacht happened a few short years later when the isolated incidents became the law in 1935.[6] It must have been a terrible

---

4 Pfennig are German currency coins of low monetary value like pennies.

5 Kristallnacht (the Night of Broken Glass) was a pogrom that took place in Germany on November 9–10, 1938, and is often seen as a turning point in Nazi policies of systematic persecution of Jews. For more information, see the glossary

6 In 1935, Nazi Germany passed the Nuremberg Laws that stripped Jews of their civil rights as German citizens and separated them from Germans legally, socially, and politically. For more information, see the glossary.

blow when Aunt Sarah and Uncle Yumi got thrown out of Germany on one hour's notice in 1938 with nothing but the clothes on their backs. They had lived there since the end of World War I, but because they had retained Polish citizenship, they were unceremoniously deposited in the border city of Zbąszyń.[7]

They came to Lodz where they had extended family, including us. I don't remember where they lived and I don't think we saw each other very often. They were devastated by having to lead our way of life. We were used to it – we'd never known any other way – but they had trouble adjusting, particularly when they had to use crude amenities like the outhouse. They considered it beneath their dignity and they sometimes resolved that problem by taking a taxi to the Grand Hotel, which had indoor plumbing.

Soon after Sarah and Yumi arrived in Lodz with nothing, my brother-in-law, Janek Ceder, undertook the unheard-of task of going to Germany to bring back some of their belongings. As incredible as it sounds, he succeeded – with the help of Herr Kaufmann, the man who had managed their store when they used to go away on their frequent holidays to spas all over Europe. He now was in complete charge of their business, compliments of the Nazis. Janek brought back a fur coat that he wore under his own coat. It's hard to imagine how he got away with it. Herr Kaufman also gave him a diamond ring that belonged to my aunt, which he brought back. We were greatly relieved when he returned unharmed. It sounds like something out of a spy story, but it is the truth. My aunt was very grateful to Herr Kaufmann for his integrity and honesty, but had no way to thank him without getting him into trouble.

My aunt coped with this situation better than her husband. In a letter that I would later receive from German-occupied Lodz while I was in the Soviet Union, she wrote that Uncle Yumi had been ad-

---

7 Known also as the *Polenaktion* or Zbąszyń deportation, the Nazi government expelled Jews of Polish origin from Germany on October 27–28, 1938.

mitted to a mental hospital. I have no idea how this letter escaped German censorship. Aunt Sarah, along with the rest of my family in Lodz, wound up in the Warsaw ghetto, not the Lodz ghetto. How this happened I will never know – I only know that it was unusual. They all disappeared without a trace.

Uncle Chaim Moshe

There is a picture that has watched over me since my days in the Soviet Union. It is the only picture I have of my family. It was taken in the village of Bolimów, about sixty kilometres from Lodz, where my father's middle brother, Chaim Moshe, lived with his large family. My family sent the photo to me from the Warsaw ghetto in the last letter I ever received from them.

One day, when I was around twelve, I was put on a hay wagon and dispatched to Bolimów for what turned out to be my only visit with Uncle Chaim Moshe. He was also a tailor, and quite poor; the whole family lived in a single room. My mother used to send the clothes that I outgrew to his family. I was a city kid, and on this visit I saw for the first time in my life how potatoes and other crops grow. When my cousins ran out, barefoot, to splash in the puddles after a heavy rain, I followed them. As a result, I came down with a deep cough and a bad cold. My relatives gave me time to recover and then I was shipped home by bus. I guess I wasn't made of the sturdy stuff that my country cousins were made of.

One of Chaim Moshe's girls, my first cousin, whose name I don't recall, once came to visit us in Lodz. I took her for a walk along the main street and she embarrassed me by talking too loudly – I constantly had to remind her to lower her voice. I guess that with a large family like hers, you had to speak up to be heard. She made me feel so cosmopolitan and urbane. It felt good to teach someone some manners and I felt very proud of myself. I never saw them again, nor do I know what happened to them. I wonder if any of them survived.

Yechiel Mayer and Other Family Members

We didn't have a large family. Both of my mother's sisters were childless and other than Uncle Chaim Moshe and his family in Bolimów, my father had one other brother, Yechiel Mayer. My uncle lived in Lodz and had an illegitimate daughter, but I didn't get to meet her until August 1939. My parents relented at that point and I was allowed to spend some time with her. I don't remember her name or what she looked like.

My uncle was a tall redhead and an excellent ladies' custom tailor. He went to France to ply his trade but the authorities there didn't look favourably on newcomers, so he came back to Lodz where his lady friend was always ready to provide him with the necessities of life. He was a real charmer and I adored him. We did have other relatives but I don't remember who they were, although I do remember that we were invited to their homes for a Sabbath meal.

Aunt Tauba and Uncle Hersh

As I've already mentioned, my mother's middle sister, Aunt Tauba, was childless. She had given birth to a baby who died in infancy. Since she had no children of her own, Tauba was very anxious for me to live with her and her husband, Hersh, at Podrzeczna No. 3. I would have my own room, a radio and other benefits that my own parents couldn't afford. It's true that there were things I wished for, like a wristwatch, which many of my affluent friends had. I had to wait until after the war to own one. Another wish I had was to have a birthday party – I had never had one of my own although I was invited to some parties. I knew that my parents couldn't afford one. I understood that my parents did the best they could with the limited means at their disposal and I never resented it. That was the same reason that I never attended a sleepover camp in summertime or even a "half-camp," which is what we called a day camp. My mother left the decision about living with my aunt and uncle to me, but she knew that I wouldn't leave my family even if my life would improve a lot.

I was too young to understand what motivated grownups some-times. For some reason Aunt Tauba hated my beloved mutt, Lord, and managed to get rid of him when I went away with my brother to a summer resort. Maybe she resented my decision not to take her up on her offer to live with her. When I found Lord gone upon my return, I couldn't understand why my mother hadn't stopped her. It may have been because we were so much poorer than Aunt Tauba and Uncle Hersh and needed their financial assistance. She also dis-posed of my precious *Kino* movie magazines. I will never know what prompted that.

Once, in our usually harmonious household, I heard my parents ar-guing. I was really surprised and lost no time in telling my Aunt Tauba about it. It was a poor decision, but I'd never heard my parent's voices raised. Tauba came right over and when she left, my father who usually called me "Chanaleh," said in a stern voice, "Chana, come here."

I didn't expect what happened next. My father took the belt off the sewing machine and hit me a couple of times on the backside. I began crying, more out of embarrassment than pain. He made me promise that I would never again tell anyone what went on in our private lives. I learned this lesson well and didn't hold it against him – he told me exactly why I was being punished. It was the only time he ever hit me.

When I came down with mumps I spent the entire time at my Aunt Tauba's flat. I slept in the living room, which suited me fine. She had recently acquired a radio and I listened to it constantly. Every day at noon I listened to the news, followed by the bugler's tune from the Mariacki Tower in Krakow. The song of the bugle always ended abruptly before it was finished. I was told that this tradition came from an old story of a bugler in the Mariacki Tower who played his bugle to warn the citizens that the Tatars were approaching, but was killed part way through.[8]

---

8 For more on the legend and the hymn – called the Mariacki Hejnał – still played today from the Mariacki Tower, see the glossary.

Sisters

Manya

I adored my sister Malka whom, as I have said, we called Manya. She truly was my role model, yet she also relied on my taste and sometimes even asked for my advice on what she should wear.

For part of my childhood, we were able to rent a summer home, usually in the spa town Ciechocinek, about 150 kilometres north of Lodz, where there were many natural mineral springs and the air smelled of iodine. There were mud and mineral baths there, too. On one occasion, before going to the cottage, my teenage sister went to visit Aunt Sarah in Berlin. When she missed the train on her return home, she was approached by two young Jewish men who offered to drive her to our cottage. She accepted their offer and when she showed up on our doorstep the next morning, after an all-night drive, my mother almost fainted. The young men complimented my mother on bringing up my sister to trust people and then they left. Looking at it from a different perspective, she was too trusting. But then again, times were different.

Shortly after we moved to Podrzeczna No. 12 in 1935 or 1936, Manya had a fateful experience. She had been loyal to the same dressmaker for a long time. But when a new one in town was highly recommended by a friend, Manya decided to give her a try. She picked up some material and took it to the new dressmaker. While she was leafing through the fashion magazines, she spied a young man in the crowd who turned out to be the dressmaker's cousin. The next time Manya returned to the dressmaker for a fitting, there he was again. It was no coincidence. He introduced himself as Janek Ceder and asked her out to the movies. Manya didn't know that at the time he was engaged to a girl from a wealthy family. When the two of them reached the box office, Janek said that he had left his wallet at home. Thinking nothing of it, my sister paid for the tickets. But he was only testing her – he had the money but wanted to know if Manya was only looking for a rich husband.

Against his parents' wishes, Janek broke off his engagement and announced plans to marry Manya. He was very well established in his own hardware business. When he asked my parents for Manya's hand in marriage, they told him that they didn't have any dowry to give. That annoyed him, but he accepted it and was well-accepted into our family. Times were changing and dowries were no longer particularly important. We presented him with a gold cigarette case and matching lighter. When Janek's mother was informed about his marriage plans, she tried to make him change them. Even though his parents were furious that he had decided to marry a girl from a poor family, he stuck to his decision.

The engagement party was held in our flat and at the next-door-neighbour's flat. It was very well attended. When my mother gave me a piece of cake and a glass of wine to take to my future brother-in-law's brother Srulek – who was known as Lulek – I didn't have enough confidence to approach him and start a conversation. After all, since I attended a school for Jewish girls, I hadn't been exposed to many boys. I must have walked around with a plate in one hand and a glass in the other for the longest time. Finally, I ate it myself while Lulek watched me in amusement. Later, when we had become friends, he constantly reminded me about it.

Janek's family consisted of five brothers. Janek (whose real name was Yoine) was the oldest, and then came Moishe, Jakub and Lulek. The fifth brother was retarded (I don't remember his name). He also had two sisters. Regina owned a small electric appliance store in Lodz and the other sister lived in Paris. They were all very good-looking, and – to the credit of their parents – they had all become independent and were able to establish businesses of their own.

I Am a Woman Now

Early one morning when I was eleven I awoke to feel someone's hand on my left shoulder, gently shaking me. I tried to shake it off, unsuccessfully. "Chanele, wake up!" It was my mother's voice. I pretended that I was still asleep, listening to the clock on the wall ticking. There was no school that day and I didn't know what the commotion was about. "Chana," my mother's voice was now getting stern, "Get up." I tried to open my sleepy eyes and look at the beautiful needlepoint on the wall next to my baby bed. Yes, my baby bed – because that's still where I slept, with my feet hanging over the edge. The tapestry had a hunting motif with white hunting dogs and beautifully dressed ladies; many times I imagined myself to be in that scene.

Having no choice, I turned over. I wasn't allowed to sleep on my left side – that was bad for the heart, my father said. So I sat up and I saw that Manya was with my mother, standing over me. I didn't know what was going on. Then I noticed that my mother was holding a pair of my panties with a brownish red blotch on them. "How did this happen?" I asked. "The stain wasn't there yesterday when I got undressed!" Maybe I hadn't looked closely enough. I wondered if this was why they were standing in front of me – in judgment over a misdemeanor of a stain. Suddenly, my mother's hand reached out and gave me a slight slap on each cheek. "Mazel tov!" she exclaimed. "You're becoming a woman!" The slap was an old Jewish custom. Next, my mother proceeded to tell me how to conduct myself on these occasions. My older sister stopped her and said, "Chana knows what is needed since I ask her sometimes to go get supplies for me."

All of a sudden, literally overnight, I was transformed from a child of eleven into a woman – from a caterpillar into a beautiful butterfly ready to spread her wings. I wasn't ready to fly yet, of course. That would come soon enough. In the meantime, I still had a few years of childhood to contend with.

Manya's Wedding

Six weeks after the engagement party, Janek and Manya got married. Aunt Sarah, the Berliner, had sent a piece of blue georgette fabric for my sister's wedding gown and a pair of silver shoes. Why the cloth was blue and not white, I'll never know. On the day of the wedding, when Manya was led to the *chuppah*, the marriage canopy, I saw that Manya's shoulders were shaking. I thought that she was crying, but when her veil was lifted, I could see that she couldn't stop laughing. As a leftist, she wasn't really keen on religion.

Janek's mother had still tried to make him change his mind even on the day of their wedding, which pushed him to cut off ties with her. It was only after their baby, Miriam, was born in early 1939 that he reconciled with his mother at my sister's insistence. Miriam was his mother's first grandchild and she adored her.

After the wedding the happy couple went off to spend their honeymoon in Zakopane, a town in southern Poland at the foot of the Tatra mountains near the Czech border. When they returned from their honeymoon, Manya gave me the boots that she had worn for skiing during the trip and a beautiful brown and gold sweater.

My family had to borrow money from Aunt Tauba's husband, Hersch, for Manya's wedding. This was ironic because when he heard that Manya was getting married he had gone berserk – it was an open secret that he was in love with her.

One Friday evening after the wedding, while we were having our dinner, Hersh showed up and demanded that we repay the debt. When my parents told him that they couldn't do it yet, he became very angry. He picked up one of our silver candlesticks and bent it out of shape. We never made an effort to straighten out that candlestick, allowing it to serve as a reminder of what jealousy can do to an otherwise nice person. To add insult to injury, the newlyweds had spent their wedding night in Hersh and Tauba's apartment.

Miriam Ceder

Manya became pregnant soon after she married but she miscarried. In the spring of 1939, however, she gave birth to a baby girl. Miriam was named after my maternal grandmother.

What can I say about my niece? Only that I adored her and looked after her. After she was born I spent more time at my sister's than I did at home. I took Miriam to the park, sang her to sleep and rocked her cradle. In my precious and only family picture, sent to me during the war, Miriam is two years old, with Shirley Temple curls, looking straight into the camera. The dress she's wearing, Manya wrote in her letter accompanying the photo, was remade for Miriam from one of mine.

Dear God,

What did she do to be deprived of life? She would have been sixty years old at the time of this writing, and probably would have been a grandmother by now.

The End of My Life in Lodz

Hollywood and Mo

I wasn't an exceptional student, but I never had to repeat a grade. In home economics I learned how to tat, embroider and knit, and the ability to knit and darn socks would later provide me with many a meal in the Soviet Union. I had developed a great fondness for the movies, mainly American ones, and my idols were Jeannette McDonald and Nelson Eddy. I never missed a single one of their movies. I'd see them again and again. I also loved Bette Davis, Joan Crawford, Deanna Durbin, Ginger Rogers and Fred Astaire, amongst others. In one of the movies I saw, it was the kitchen that impressed me most and I promised myself that one day I would live in a house with such a kitchen.

As I entered my teen years, I started noticing the opposite sex. My brother-in-law's middle brother – Lulek – had come to visit us one day wearing a Polish army uniform. He looked incredibly handsome and I fell in love with him – or maybe it was the uniform that did it. He was very good-natured and attentive to me. Once, after attending a film, we came out into the cold and he pulled my collar up to keep me warm. I liked being cared for and I think that were it not for the war, we would probably have gotten married. Everybody else thought so too.

In the early fall of 1938, my father bought a piece of navy blue cloth to make me a winter coat and we took it to a custom tailor on our street. During one of the fittings, he marked the buttonholes with a piece of chalk and touched my private parts. At first I thought it was my imagination, but it happened a second time, this time with more pressure. For the last fitting, I asked my father to come with me without telling him the reason. Maybe it was accidental, I thought, after all, the coat-maker was a poor, religious man with a large family.

The coat turned out very well. It was trimmed with a grey Persian lamb collar and lapels and six beautiful buttons. One day, coming home from school, I was attacked by a young Pole who twisted all the buttons off my coat and ran away. That scared me terribly. It was the first time I had ever experienced anything like that. When I came home, shaken, my father wanted to replace the buttons with the same ones, but I insisted upon plain ones. One experience like that was enough. I wore that coat in Russia until I grew out of it; by then, all the buttons were gone.

The Last Dayenu

In the spring of 1939 the annual rites of the season began as they did every year when the housewives dumped the old straw from the mattresses and replaced it with fresh smelling straw. This meant that Passover couldn't be far off.

For Passover, I was always outfitted with new clothing – new ribbons for my braids, new underwear and socks, a dress and new shoes. My mother always took me shopping, but in the spring of 1939, she couldn't spare the time. We had an addition in our family. My twenty-three-year-old sister had just given birth to her baby girl – Miriam – making me an aunt at almost fourteen. My mother was busy helping my sister cope with the baby.

The task of buying me shoes fell to my Aunt Tauba. Aunt Sarah had been thrown out of Germany the year before and had enough problems of her own – she didn't participate in our Passover preparations this year. Upon entering the shoe store my aunt immediately asked for a pair of flat, black patent-leather shoes with a strap, the kind I had worn since the age of five. My eyes were drawn to a pair of blue suede pumps trimmed with pink leather criss-crosses and – most importantly – a three-centimetre heel. My mind was made up: I had to have those shoes. After all, at my age I wanted to make my own selection. A battle of wills ensued – it was to be those shoes or none. My aunt got annoyed with me, but I emerged victorious, much to the delight of my sister, who applauded me for asserting my independence. My sister loved my beautiful new shoes and since we were the same size, she wore them sometimes too.

Preparations for Passover could be seen and felt everywhere. The wooden floor of our kitchen – which was where my father worked as well as where my mother cooked – was scoured with sand to get out the oil stains left by the sewing machines. Red wax was applied to the floor and allowed to dry. Finally, a heavy polisher was pushed manually across the floor to give it a shine. My mother distilled homemade wine, drop after drop running through clean linen, leaving a deposit. The linen was changed a few times until the wine was clear. She also prepared a large jar of cut-up red beets and water – the water would ferment and be used in place of vinegar, which wasn't allowed because it is a product of wheat, or *chametz*, which is forbidden on Passover, and the beets were used for our borsht (beet soup). Our large laundry basket, by now well scrubbed and lined with a large white sheet, was ready to store the matzah (unleavened bread). We had special Passover dishes and cutlery, but we didn't have a Passover set of pots and pans so our everyday set was made kosher by a man who pulled a wagon containing metal vats with hot water. After the pots and pans were dipped in the water, the cookware was declared kosher for Passover.[1]

---

1 During Passover, Jews refrain from eating *chametz* – that is, anything that contains leavened wheat, barely, rye, oats, and spelt. In preparation for the holiday,

After all these preparations, we followed our father through the house on the evening before Passover. With candles in our hands – he held a feather – we went through every corner to get out the last bits of *chametz* trapped in the crevices. We would follow the tradition of burning any last *chametz* we found the next morning.

By noon the next day, everything was ready for the festivities. The beautifully ironed white tablecloth, the polished sterling silver candlesticks, the armchair where my father would sit leaning on a huge pillow at the first seder that evening. On the table were china, cutlery, napkins, wine glasses and a plate of matzah covered with a beautifully embroidered cover set before my father's seat. A traditional round seder plate held a roasted egg, a shank bone, bitter herbs and so on.[2] Mouth-watering smells emanated from the kitchen all afternoon. My stomach growled, but it would have to wait. My sister, her husband and the baby soon arrived. There were six adults, but only four chairs. The lounge was put against the table for me and my brother, Shoel.

The seder began when the women lit the candles, said the blessings and the Haggadot were opened. My brother asked the Four Questions, even though I was the youngest (except for the baby). I checked Elijah's cup to see if he had drunk from it. The seder prayers

---

they also carefully remove these foods and any food that has come in contact with them from their homes in an annual cleaning spree and prepare foods that don't contain *chametz* – such as matzah, unleavened bread. They either use a separate set of dishes and cookware that have never come into contact with *chametz* and are only used at this time of the year, or dishes that have been specially cleaned before the holiday begins. For more information on Passover observances, see the glossary.

2 A seder is the ritual family meal celebrated on the first two nights of Passover at which the story of the Jews' exodus from Egypt is recounted. It is customary for the man of the house to lead the seder while leaning or reclining on cushions, a tradition that is meant to underline the freedom of those participating in contrast to the Jewish slaves in Egypt. The seder plate is a special plate containing six symbolic foods used by Jews during the Passover seder. For more information, see the glossary.

and readings went smoothly until we reached the song "Dayenu."[3] As long as I could remember I always giggled when I heard this song. This year, I was almost fourteen years old and an aunt and I hoped that I had outgrown the laughing. No such luck. As we got closer to singing "Dayenu" my father's blue eyes beneath bushy black brows fixed on me as if asking me to behave. I got up from the table, my hand over my mouth, and when I reached the kitchen the giggles I was holding back erupted. A short time later I rejoined the family. The *afikoman* was on top of the wardrobe and easy to find. [4] My sister, her husband and the baby left quite late.

I had trouble falling asleep that night. I was waiting for the morning to arrive so I could put on all my new clothes and impress my friends. The aroma from the kitchen woke me up. My mother was preparing breakfast for me. It wasn't very fancy – during Passover she served either *matzah brie* or *bubbaleh* with lots of eggs.[5] In those days we didn't worry about cholesterol. Tea with lemon followed. My special treat was sponge cake with wine. Pouring the wine over the cake, I waited for the liquid to be absorbed. It tasted heavenly, just like

---

3 The Haggadah (plural: Haggadot) is a book of readings and prayers used by participants at a Passover seder. The asking of the Four Questions in the Haggadah – beginning with "why is this night different from other nights" – is one of the most important rituals of the seder. Usually asked by the youngest child at the table, the seder readings that follow are answers to the questions and tell the story of the Exodus. Elijah's cup is a cup of wine customarily set apart on the seder table in honor of the prophet Elijah. "Dayenu" is a traditional and upbeat song of gratitude sung at the seder that lists the many gifts given by God to the Jewish people. It has a repetitive chorus loved by children.

4 The *afikoman* is a half-piece of matzah which is broken in the early stages of the seder and set aside to be eaten after the meal. It is usually hidden by the seder leader and children are encouraged to try to find it as part of a game to keep them interested in the seder. For more information, see the glossary.

5 *Matzah brie* is dish made of pieces of matzah dipped in eggs and fried, *bubbaleh* is a kind of light pancake made of eggs, sugar and matzah meal.

a torte. After breakfast I joined my girlfriends in the courtyard. We played some hopscotch and my new shoes got scuffed, but a brush with special bristles quickly fixed them.

Aunt Sarah came to join us for lunch. Afterward she took me to see a movie, *The Great Waltz*, a popular American film made in 1938. My aunt was a very attractive woman in her forties. Beautifully dressed, she drew admiring glances from the holiday crowd filling the main streets on this warm, sunny spring day full of promise. On the way home we passed Rumba, the new ice-cream parlour. It was crowded and I was tempted to go in, but I resisted it. I remember being so proud walking beside Sarah. I didn't want the day to end, but it was getting late and the preparations for the second seder were in full swing. I wondered how I would react to "Dayenu" that night. To tell the truth, I don't remember. It would be many years before I heard "Dayenu" again. By then, I didn't find the song funny.

On the Eve of War

Before I knew it, it was the late spring of 1939 and my formal seventh grade of education was coming to an end. I cashed in the savings stamps that I had accumulated at school and decided to buy myself some new clothes once school was out. On the last day of school I bought some flowers to present to my favourite teacher. I don't remember which teacher it was, but I do recall the gesture. I received my *censura*, my final report card, and said good bye to my friends. I promised to meet them in the fall, little knowing that Hitler had other plans in store for us. I leisurely walked home, making no plans for the future. I had enough time, I thought, to decide.

I used up everything I had accumulated from my school saving stamps and treated myself to a pair of shoes with elevated heels, a matching purse, a pair of gloves, a short houndstooth jacket, a navy blue skirt, a navy beret and silk stockings – my very first pair! Shopping on my own gave me the greatest thrill. At school we had worn only uniforms. Mine was navy blue satin with a white collar. The elbows constantly wore out, so my father made a shield to pull over the sleeves to make them last longer. I put away my purchases to wear in the fall, for Rosh Hashanah. Unfortunately, it wasn't meant to be. I never got the chance to wear my new clothes.

That same summer, Manya rented a cottage in Wiśniowa Góra, which means Cherry Hill in English, and I spent some time with her there. It wasn't too far from Lodz, so my brother-in-law came almost every night. Aunt Sarah also came to visit. Since they could afford it my sister also hired a woman to look after the baby.

When I returned to Lodz in mid-August 1939, just two weeks before the war started, I found to my dismay that my parents had moved again. As fate would have it, it would be for the last time. I was very unhappy about the move, particularly because it was unexpected and I was now further away from all my friends.

The new apartment was in a better part of the city, though, with a balcony facing the street. It was one large room that we divided with a partition. One side served as my father's small work area – by that time, my father only employed two workers and himself. The other side served as our living quarters. We finally had indoor plumbing – no more outhouses. The only furniture we still had was two beds, a table and some chairs. Our beautiful wardrobe that held so many memories was long gone. After more than twenty-five years of marriage my parents ended up exactly as they had started, with very little. Even that would be taken away, along with their lives. In August 1939, my mother was fifty-three; my father fifty-two.

War and Occupation

Our lives changed abruptly in the fourth week of August 1939 when a loud knock at the door woke us up at five o'clock in the morning. It was one of my father's employees letting us know that he wouldn't be coming to work – the government had announced a mobilization and he had been called up; he was being sent to the border.[5] After he left, I opened the balcony door and stepped outside. I saw a lot of movement, mostly men in uniform on horseback and in horse-drawn carriages setting out to fight the enemy. Even at my age I could see that they were going to be sitting ducks. The newsreels and the newspapers told us how well the Germans were prepared. They had already occupied Czechoslovakia and claimed Austria as their own without firing a single shot.[6] The Germans knew that they couldn't fail because the rest of the world had turned a blind eye to what was going on.

When my brother-in-law, Janek, was called up, we faced a serious problem. He had decided to sell his hardware store in Lodz that summer and relocate to the nearby smaller town of Koluszki, about twenty kilometres east, but he had received his draft orders before he could close the deal. My sister went to the authorities to explain that he was in Koluszki, but they assumed it was an excuse and that he was planning to desert, so they gave him twenty-four hours' notice to show up or face court martial. Luckily, Manya was able to get in touch with him. He came to say good-bye, wearing a uniform, and that was the last time we saw him. We later heard rumours that he had been taken as a prisoner of war on the outskirts of Warsaw and shipped to a camp in Romania. But there was no way to know for sure.

September 1, 1939 arrived and the Nazis started sealing the fate of European Jewry. Murder and unimaginable horrors were in store for us. The city was actually very quiet – the calm before the storm – ex-

---

5 The Polish government only announced a mobilization on August 30, 1939, two days before the German invasion, having mistakenly calculated that the Germans wouldn't attack before 1942.

6 Germany invaded Austria in March 1938 and quickly annexed the country to the Third Reich. At the end of September 1938, after months of international diplomatic crisis, Germany occupied and annexed the Sudeten area of Czechoslovakia. In January 1939 the rest of Czechoslovakia was occupied by Germany.

cept for newsboys shouting, "Extra!" and proclaiming that Poland was preparing Hitler's coffin to bury him. Everyone said that with England and France on our side, it was going to be a short war.[7] We read in the newspapers that the Germans were shooting with ersatz ammunition, and that it was up to Poland to finish the beast. Nevertheless, we started buying up food and other supplies.

Then, in the days immediately before the Germans entered Lodz, the looting of stores began, particularly Jewish and liquor stores. My sister's store was no exception, even though there wasn't much to steal since most of the merchandise had already been moved to Koluszki. We decided to close up our apartment and move in with Manya. We didn't know what the next day was going to bring, but we had a premonition of things to come. We grew closer to each other, as if there was safety in numbers.

Lodz wasn't bombed at all, but for days, every time we looked up at the sky there were hundreds of German planes flying on their way to bomb Warsaw into surrender. The weather was perfect for flying and bombing accurately and the invaders took advantage of it. Soon the capital city was under siege.

Panic broke out as news of the Germans approaching Lodz reached us. People started leaving the city by the thousands by whatever means possible. We wanted to go, but our father, intent on keeping the family together, wouldn't let us. He may have been right to make us stay. All those poor people ended up trapped outside the city and were bombed mercilessly by low-flying planes; dead bodies littered the highways. There was nowhere to run.

A week of uncertainty ended when German troops marched into Lodz on Friday, September 8, 1939. It was a warm, sunny day and I

---

7 Poland had signed military alliances with France and Great Britain prior to 1939. As a result, when the Germans attacked on September 1, 1939, both these powers – along with Australia, New Zealand, South Africa and Canada – declared war on Germany on September 3, 1939.

walked toward Plac Wolności to watch the arrival of the occupiers. They came on foot and in trucks, looking immaculate in their uniforms, boots shining. Many of them carried flowers from the German population of the city. City Hall and other buildings were decked out with huge flags with swastikas. In other words, the city rolled out the red carpet to welcome the invaders, whom some regarded as liberators. The large German population of the city opened their arms for their brethren, even though the community had lived in Poland for generations.[8] There weren't many sad faces in the throngs, and there were fewer Jews.

Signs of things to come appeared almost immediately. I witnessed a soldier pulling an elderly Jewish man's beard and kicking him to the ground because he wasn't working fast enough to fill the trenches that had been dug only a few days before to stop the German tanks. I remember how enthusiastic and patriotic we had felt when we dug those trenches.

At the end of September, after weeks of siege and relentless bombing, Warsaw capitulated and the triumphant German army occupied the city on October 1, 1939. In the conquered capital city, burned out, demolished buildings bore witness to the results of modern warfare.[9] A beautiful, cultural city was reduced to rubble. Most of Warsaw's defenders were dead, and while the valiant survivors could resist no longer they were still full of spirit.

My sister's store faced the Zielong Rynek, the Green Market. On one Sunday soon after the Germans arrived, the stalls in the market were closed and some boys were playing soccer there when a truck

---

8 Lodz's ethnic German population made up approximately 10 per cent of the total population of the city before the war. For more information on ethnic Germans, see *Volsdeutsche* in the glossary.

9 The 1939 Battle of Warsaw started with huge aerial bombardments by the Luftwaffe starting on September 1, 1939; land fighting started on September 8 and the city was soon under siege. The siege lasted until September 28.

with German soldiers went by. They stopped and joined the boys in the game, which frightened everybody. Another time, when I took my niece for a stroll in the park – this was before the harsh laws banning us from parks were passed – an older soldier next to me started playing with Miriam. With tears in his eyes, he told me that he had left a baby the same age back in Germany. I don't remember any other demonstrations of kindness. Maybe the same soldier would think nothing of bashing a Jewish baby's head against a wall to kill it. These examples are just too minor when you consider what was about to happen to us.

The Germans dynamited the monument to the Polish hero Tadeusz Kosciusko at the centre of Plac Wolności as soon as they entered Lodz. I remember walking by one day and seeing it lying on the ground. Its head was separated from the torso and a victorious German soldier was having his picture taken with his arm around his girlfriend and his foot on Kosciusko's head.

Before long, all kinds of decrees and restrictions started appearing, each one more dehumanizing than the last.[10] There were so many of them that it's hard to remember them all, although a few stand out in my memory. No Jews were allowed to attend school or institutes of higher learning, regardless of age, which brought my formal education to an end at fourteen. We were banned from using public transportation and from entering any park, theatre or cinema. A curfew was imposed from seven at night until seven in the morning. We had to get off the sidewalk when a German soldier approached. Most shameful of all, we had to wear an armband as a sign of our

---

10 On November 7, 1939, Lodz was incorporated into the Third Reich and the Nazis changed its name to Litzmannstadt. The measures imposed by the Germans to strip Jews of all legal, economic and social rights, some already implemented within days of the occupation, were now intensified. The next several months also saw daily roundups of Jews for forced labour, random beatings and killings on the streets.

Jewish identity on our sleeves. Disobeying this rule was punishable by death.[11]

It wasn't safe for a male Jew of any age to be in the street. They were constantly being caught and put to work in forced labour, whether the Germans needed them or not. One of them was my father. We didn't see him once for a whole day and were very relieved when he came home with a loaf of bread after working in a bakery.

One evening, just before the curfew, I was walking home past the Deutsche Shul after visiting a girlfriend and saw a big crowd gathered. I stopped and watched in horror as soldiers rolled in barrels full of tar and set the building on fire.[12]

"It's a great day," gloated one Pole.

"Don't be so happy," warned his friend. "They will start with the Jews, and finish with the Poles."

I couldn't stay too long to eavesdrop because it was so close to curfew. When I went past the synagogue the next day, there was nothing left except the lingering smell of the fire. Another sign of things to come.

There was a public hanging of a Jewish man named Radner and two Polish men in the poor Jewish section of Lodz. Although the bodies were on display for some time, I wasn't allowed to go see them. I don't know what their crimes were. In Radner's case, it may have been that he wasn't wearing his armband, or some other similar "heinous" crime.

The bread lines were now longer and whenever a Jew got to the front of the line, he or she was pointed out and sent back to the

---

11 On November 16, 1939, Jews were ordered to wear an armband on their right arm, the precursor to the yellow Star of David badge that followed on December 12, 1939. By then, Ann had already left Lodz.

12 All the synagogues of Lodz were set on fire and completely destroyed by the Germans in November 1939. The Deutsche Shul (Great Synagogue) was burned to the ground on the night of November 14–15, 1939, along with its Torah scrolls and interior fixtures.

end. Many times people went home without any bread. Some Jews thought they didn't look Jewish and didn't wear the armbands, putting themselves in terrible danger. Even if the Germans couldn't identify them, the Poles had no trouble spotting them and pointing them out. Sometimes I was able to get in line by four o'clock in the morning and, with any luck, came home with bread.

Any kind of social life stopped for us altogether. Our radios had been confiscated immediately after the Germans occupied Lodz. Ours had been a beautiful Philips short-wave radio with a "magic eye," a cathode tube for adjusting the station. I missed being able to listen to the music from France, the international news from Moscow, or short wave broadcasts from the United States – even though I didn't understand what they were saying. All of the newspapers except German ones published in Polish had been shut down. My favourite had been *Express*. The curfew kept us from venturing out from early evening until morning, so we were left with each other for company. Our only joy was watching little Miriam, who at six months old was a delight. We hadn't heard any news from Malka's husband.

Poland's independence, which had lasted between the two world wars, was now ended. Germany occupied most of the western part of Poland and, because of the pact between the Soviet Union and Germany signed by Soviet minister Vyacheslav Mikhailovich Molotov and German foreign minister Joachim von Ribbentrop earlier in 1939, the Soviets now occupied the eastern part.[13] For a brief period in 1939, the Germans allowed people to cross into the eastern parts of pre-war Poland now under Soviet administration. A steady exodus started, and my brother, Shoel, along with a few friends, decided to join the mass of people fleeing. Just a few days after leaving, however, Shoel returned home minus the gold watch and money that had been taken

---

13 The USSR invaded Poland on September 17, 1939, in keeping with the secret terms of the Treaty of Non-aggression (colloquially known as the Molotov-Ribbentrop Pact) signed with Germany in late August 1939. For more information, see the glossary.

as payment by a guide who promptly disappeared. When Shoel returned home, we were relieved to be a family again and face our fate together.

But the situation in Lodz was getting worse every day, so my brother decided to give it another try. His intent this time was to go to Soviet-occupied Bialystok, some 330 kilometres to the northeast, find a place to stay and then come back for the rest of the family. As things turned out his plan was impossible. My parents wouldn't leave Manya alone with baby Miriam and she had decided to stay in Lodz until she heard from her husband. As November 1939 drew to a close, my brother decided he would go alone. I, however, had a plan of my own – I wanted to go with him. For some reason, my parents didn't object. Did they have a premonition?

Shoel and I were ready to leave at the end of November, taking quite a bit of luggage with us. A horse-drawn carriage was called to take us to the railroad station and we said tearful goodbyes, not realizing that it would be the last time we'd ever see each other. We kissed for the last time and went out into the cold, dark night to face the unknown. As I entered the carriage, I heard my mother calling me. She rushed out of the house, took the pink wool shawl off her shoulders and wrapped it around me. She kissed me again and said the words that I would always remember: "Be decent."

I stuck to these principles in spite of terrible difficulties. I would have made her proud had she known. I was good and decent, but at what price? I was rewarded with years of hunger, loneliness and homelessness. And yet, I always felt her protective arms around me. Even though her woolen pink shawl was later stolen, it kept me warm – if only in the abstract. She kept watch over me.

There would be no more listening to family stories, no more bananas or mandarins when I was sick. No more being blessed every night before bedtime. No more goodnight kiss.

From now on, life for me was going to be serious business, just trying to survive. As we were pulled away from our home, I turned for the last time to see my mother. She was wiping her eyes and waving. I waved back until we disappeared from each other's view. The truth is that I didn't feel apprehension about leaving. I was excited and ready for the first adventure of my life. But as it turned out, my happy and carefree childhood was over. I just didn't know it yet.

Into the Unknown

Leaving Poland

As of this moment, our lives took a different direction and took on a different dimension, away from the loving arms of our family. We got on a train to Warsaw via Koluszki, which was a major railway junction. On the trip we were subjected to a lot of antisemitic verbal abuse from Poles on the train. They didn't allow us into any of the compartments, which meant that we had to either sit or stand on the floor of the corridor. They didn't blame the German occupiers for the war – they blamed us. They seemed to be quite content with the present state of affairs. For the first time in my young life I was truly frightened and sorry that I had embarked on this adventure. But it was too late to turn back.

When we arrived in Warsaw we had to wait hours for a connecting train to take us to the border city of Malkinia Górna. I sat on the floor, afraid to move or attract undue attention, getting dirty looks from the Poles, who, rather than being hateful toward the invaders of the country, vented their hostility on us. It was a completely new experience for me. Until now I had been surrounded almost exclusively by Jews.

There were many German soldiers patrolling the railroad station, but two of them stand out in my memory. In shining boots and pressed uniforms and tidy all over they were walking along leisurely whistling the "Beer Barrel Polka" in harmony.[1] It was the first time I'd heard this tune. I memorized it well and even now, whenever I hear it, I see that long-ago scene at the Warsaw railroad station again.

In the morning we got on the train along with hundreds of other people, mostly Jews. We were packed in like sardines, a foretaste of things to come for the people who chose to remain in German-occupied territory and who were later shipped to concentration and death camps like cattle. The only difference was that they were going in a different direction, toward death.

When we reached Malkinia Górna on the new German-Soviet border, panic ensued as women and men were separated by the German border police. I was afraid that I would never see my brother again. German border police with large dogs on leashes chased us for a few kilometres to a checkpoint where we were reunited with the men. A very long line formed and the Germans started checking everybody and everything that people had with them, things like pots, pans, pillows and down comforters. Many things were confiscated and left behind. In the process, some people got terrible beatings because they weren't moving fast enough. The Germans had put the most rabidly vicious enforcers on the border to handle the crowds of frightened people that came through every day. A young man ahead of me in line was so scared and shaking that he dropped his papers – he was beaten so badly that I didn't see him get up. The line couldn't be held up and soon my turn came.

The German border policeman asked me if I had any money and I handed him the twenty-zloty bill that my mother had given me for emergencies. Unknown to me, she had also sewn four more bills into the hem of my skirt. I'm not sure how I would have re-

---

1   In English, this song is better known as "Roll out the Barrel." It became very popular around the world during World War II.

acted had I known about it, so she was wise not to have told me. The German took the bill, and to my surprise, tore it in half and put it in his pocket. We were chased to another checkpoint where this time an official barked at me. "Are you carrying any ammunition or guns?" I was stunned and numb with terror. Finally, we got through and had to run the last few hundred metres to cross into the Soviet Union's newly acquired territory.

We were free.

Bialystok

Once we had crossed the border checkpoint on the German-occupied side, there was a no-man's land where thousands of people waited for days to be allowed into the Soviet Union. Shoel and I were among the few lucky ones to get through with little delay. Many people got discouraged waiting and the cold, hunger and lack of money forced them to go back into the beasts' den and the fate awaiting them there.

We crossed into Soviet territory when we found a ride from a peasant with a hay wagon who took as many as he could accommodate – for pay, of course – to the home of a woman who fed us and put us up for the night in her cellar. In the middle of the night, we heard Soviet soldiers coming to look for refugees to take them back to the German side. Apparently the border was only officially open at certain times and we had crossed illegally. The soldiers didn't look in the cellar, though, having been assured there was nobody there.

We were safe for the time being. Early the next morning we started out on the last leg of our trip – to the railway station at Zareby Kościelne, a previously Polish town that was now under Soviet control, and from there hopefully on to Bialystok. Only one pregnant woman was allowed to ride on the peasant's wagon. The rest of us had to make the cold, slippery walk to the train station a few kilometres away hanging on to the sides to keep from falling down.

When the train finally arrived it was a scramble to get on. Anyone left behind would have to wait until the next day. We made it on board even though we had to stand the whole way. There wasn't room to move. I don't remember how long it took for the train to get to Bialystok, but when we arrived we were greeted by the sight of a lot of Soviet soldiers and red flags everywhere at the railroad station. They gave us hot tea, sugar cubes and bread. The apprehension and disbelief I felt at first slowly disappeared and I began to feel protected.

We still had to find a place to stay. At first, we stayed with a Jewish family, but that only lasted until our money ran out. I have to, unfortunately, be honest here: Bialystok's Jewish population didn't look very favourably on this wave of refugees. They didn't know – nor did we – that in two short years they too would suffer the fate of other Jews, and by then they would have no place to run.

With no money, we had no choice but to join others in seeking refuge in one of the synagogues. It was mid-December and the synagogue was unheated, so to keep ourselves warm we started burning the wooden seats. The conditions were awful. There was no place to wash clothes and the toilets were overflowing. Most of us became infested with lice and spent our time picking the lice off our clothing since we had nothing else to do.

One day we ran into Manya's father-in-law and two of his sons, Moishe and Jakub. Jakub still looked gorgeous in his Polish Army uniform. They told us that they had decided to go back to Lodz because they couldn't stand the hardships of refugee life in Bialystok. They wanted to go back to the rest of their family and face the future together. My brother begged me to go back with them. Tempting as it was to go off with this gorgeous guy, I refused. If it meant going back to Lodz, it was no contest. Here I was, having the adventure of a lifetime, and I wasn't going to give it up.

Not one single member of the Ceder family survived.

The Red Miracle

After more than four weeks of squatting in the synagogue, the Soviets presented us – along with all the refugees from western Poland – with an option: we could choose to become Soviet citizens and stay on this side of the new border or we could return to German-occupied Poland, meaning we could go back to Lodz.[2] When the Soviets opened a new opportunity for refugees to register to work as volunteers for one year, Shoel and I decided to take that option. We thought we would be able to wait out what we all still hoped would be a short war. The Soviets had already begun this new program to send refugees to the Russian interior, where workers were desperately needed.

Once Shoel and I had officially volunteered, the Soviet authorities treated us well: we were given a place to stay a few kilometres from the city while we waited for an *echelon*, a transport, to take us on our journey. It looked like a summer camp and, looking back now, it probably was. We joined a group of Polish Jewish refugees there who had all volunteered to work. We slept on mattresses and the place was heated. The Red Army soldiers kept us entertained and the Soviet authorities fed us until a train became available to take us to our then-unknown destination. When we received the news about where we were going and what the detail was to be, it was welcome. We were to be assigned to work at a brick-making factory. Those of us who weren't yet sixteen years of age would be sent to school. I was still only fourteen years old.

---

2 Many of the Polish Jews in Soviet territory at this time, faced with the terrible hardships of life as homeless refugees, elected to return to German-occupied Poland. The Soviets knew that the Germans wouldn't accept them back and soon arrested them – for having "demonstrated disloyalty." In June 1940, most of these refugees were deported by the Soviets into remote areas to do forced labour. Inadvertently, this saved them – most refugees who opted to become Soviet citizens and stayed in the Soviet zone of pre-war Poland were killed when the Germans invaded in June 1941.

At last, we were going to begin our journey into a new and unfamiliar life. It was January 6, 1940.

Crossing Soviet Russia

On the day of our departure we boarded the train, which was a modified cattle car transport. Each car was equipped with a wood-burning stove for heating as well as for warming food or boiling water. We slept on boards – I don't remember if we had any mattresses or blankets. We were very crowded and that was what kept us warm. I slept next to my brother.

Early on in the journey I woke up in the middle of the night sensing someone's presence standing over me. I was sleeping at the edge of the bunk and, sure enough, I could make out his face. It was the *feldsher*, the medic. He was a middle-aged man, what we would now call a child molester. He ran his hands up my leg and I pushed him away. He left without saying one word. I never mentioned this incident to my brother and, fortunately, two brothers from Warsaw moved into the bunks next to us, which gave me more protection at night.

The *feldsher* was in charge of the hospital car. There were no other doctors or medics on the train and he looked after hundreds of people. It wasn't a scheduled train and sometimes it ran for hours non-stop. Other times we had to wait until a track opened for us to continue. When the train stopped abruptly, whatever was on the wood-burning stove turned over and anyone unlucky enough to be nearby got burned. I was assigned to help the *feldsher* in treating the victims – I'm sure that he had something to do with me being given this assignment. The hospital car was somewhat more comfortable, but I had to help him apply dressings to the burns that many people got from the boiling water. The injuries were very severe and I was exposed to a lot of suffering. It was at times like these that I wished I was back in the other car with the rest of the passengers.

When the train ran all day, the men had no problem when it came to urinating. They just opened the doors a bit, stood on the edge and peed. The yellow stream practically froze in mid-air, sometimes freezing on the doorframes so that the doors wouldn't shut properly and the frigid air then blew right into the car. Whenever this happened, we would have to boil water and pour it onto the side of the doorframe to melt the frozen urine. It was much worse for women. We had to use any pot we could find and then dump the contents through the door. Again, water had to be poured to melt the ice and keep people from freezing. There was absolutely no such thing as privacy.

A few times, in the larger cities, we were given an opportunity to go to a *banya*, a bathhouse, and to have our clothing deloused. As improbable as it sounds, the *banya* attendants for men were women, and for women, men. Personally, I think that the *disinfektsiya*, the disinfectant, they used actually helped the lice to multiply because the process wasn't hot enough.

By now it was mid-January and I still didn't know how much further we were going. When we reached the Ural Mountains that separated Europe from Asia, Comrade Maslov, our transport's leader, explained to us where we were. There was only a small, barely visible plaque marking the place. I was disappointed because I thought it ought to be bigger. At one of our stops along the way, my brother and a few other young men missed the train. In this vast country I was afraid I might never see him again, but, much to our relief, they somehow caught up with us.

After travelling more than 1,500 kilometres, we reached Chelyabinsk, just east of the Ural Mountains, and then went another 1,400 kilometres east to Novosibirsk. From there it was another two hundred kilometres south to Barnaul on the Ob River and finally, at last, another four hundred kilometres to our ultimate destination – Ridder/Leninogorsk.[3]

---

3 By the time, Ann reached Ridder/Leninogorsk, she had traveled more than 4,500 kilometres from Bialystok. See maps on page 186–187.

Ridder/Leninogorsk

On February 2, 1940, we reached the city of Ridder/Leninogorsk, which is in eastern Kazakhstan in Siberia, only about five hundred kilometres from the Chinese border. It had taken a month to get there. The city was named for an Englishman, Phillip Ridder, who found a rich metal deposit there in 1786. After the Germans invaded the Soviet Union in 1941, the Soviets renamed it Leninogorsk, but we always referred to it as Ridder.[4]

As soon as we arrived, our transport was met by Soviet officials who divided the volunteers into three groups. The first group, consisting of married couples, was given a dormitory in the city of Ridder. Families got larger accommodations in centrally heated buildings. My group of twenty-four single women was taken to the so-called First Region, seven kilometres from the city, while the group of thirty-six single men was given a dorm further away in the Second Region. There were more single men because girls had generally chosen to stay with their families in Poland. We all kept in touch with each other. When we went to visit, we had to go on foot because there was no public transportation.

I shared a room with a few girls. Gienia Kaliner took a bed near the door. Also with us were Gienia Naihaus, Eva Goldberg and Eva Lillienheim (Eva 1 and Eva 2, as we called them), Lena Feinberg, Hela Szynes and Paula Lubinsky. From time to time we alternated rooms and ended up with some of the other girls from the larger group of volunteers. Most of them were from Warsaw and the surrounding area. What a luxury it was to have my own bed with a clean straw

---

4 The town kept the name Leninogorsk from 1941 until 2002, when it reverted to its original name, Ridder. The term Siberia broadly refers to the region that extends eastward from the Ural Mountains to the Pacific coast, and southward from the Arctic Ocean to the hills of north-central Kazakhstan and the national borders of both Mongolia and China.

mattress, a pillow with a pillowcase and a blanket! The room was kept warm by a Russian attendant. After one day of rest we were put to work, mostly in construction. Like Comrade Lenin said, "One who doesn't work doesn't eat."

I didn't actually end up staying with this group for very long because I was one of the youngest in the group and, according to Soviet law, I had to attend school until the age of sixteen. I was only fourteen and a half. One day in mid-February 1940 they removed me from my assigned job of painting the walls of the communal bathhouse before I'd even held a brush in my hand. Instead I was taken in an official black car to a dormitory that belonged to a *Tekhnikum* – a technical and vocational school – and given a room to share with two other Russian girls. I was given a scholarship – a *stipenda* – and got on with my education.

Ridder had an immense lead mine and the school specialized in metallurgical sciences and trained engineers and technicians. We took physics, metallurgy and other courses, all in Russian of course. I didn't find the language too difficult to learn, even though the Cyrillic alphabet was different from the Latin characters used for Polish. Soon my brother was also admitted to the school and it seemed that my life was shaping up quite well. Things were beginning to look up. Even the war seemed remote. All we needed was our family to complete the picture.

The school's secretary, a Polish woman named Natalia Petrovna Makovskaya, took me under her wing almost as soon as I arrived. She and her husband were ardent communists who had decided to come live in the Soviet Union during World War I. On February 23, Red Army Day, she made me write a speech in Polish that she translated into Russian for the students' assembly.[5] I remember clearly that in my speech I told the students what they wanted to hear and what

---

5 Red Army Day was a holiday that honoured all those who served or were serving in the Soviet Union's armed forces. For more information, see the glossary.

my sister, Manya, had once told me. "The Soviet Union has lost one day per week," I proclaimed. "This is because people work five days a week and have free time every sixth day – and it always fells on a different day of the week!" This got me a big laugh as well as applause.

My next engagement was on March 8, International Women's Day.[6] After only two short weeks, I was now able to utter a few sentences in Russian. By May 1, May Day, I no longer needed to have my speech translated.[7] My transition into the new language was very smooth.

The first class I was put in was only for beginners, to prepare us for the first year of the *Tekhnikum* program. The students were a mixture of Kazakhs, Russians, Ukrainians and me, the only Jewish student. Even though we were in Kazakhstan, there weren't many native students – the locals were mostly Muslim and used Arabic script, or were members of nomadic and Turkic tribes; some were Buddhists or practitioners of other faiths.

There were many Ukrainians in Ridder because they had been exiled to Siberia in the 1930s after being categorized as *kulaks*, which was the word the Soviets used for prosperous or landowning peasants. Their land was taken away from them during the period of collectivization to form *kolkhozy* (collective farms) or *sovkhozy* (large state-owned farms) and they were deprived of their rights as Soviet citizens.[8] They were only recognized again after the outbreak of the German-Soviet war, when soldiers were needed, a fate that also awaited people of other nationalities who had been mistreated by Stalin.

---

6   International Women's Day was declared a holiday by the first international women's conference in 1910 and became a holiday in Russia in 1917. Celebrated around the world on March 8, it marks the struggle for equal rights for women.

7   Also known as International Workers' Day, May Day is celebrated on May 1 in many countries around the world in recognition of the achievements of workers and the international labour movement. For more information, see the glossary.

8   Collectivization was the policy pursued in the Soviet Union after 1929 to forcibly reorganize agriculture by expropriating land into state ownership or creating

I met a Jewish family in Ridder, the Cygelmans, whose daughter worked at the school office as a secretary. She introduced me to her family and I was invited every Friday night to have dinner with them. The menu was chicken soup with noodles and gefilte fish. I think that they invited me in part because of my ability to darn socks, the craft I learned at school in Lodz. The Cygelmans had piles of socks that needed to be darned, which provided me with many Friday night dinners. That would come to an end when the Soviet Union entered the war in 1941 and their two sons were called to defend their country. After that there were no more socks to darn except their father's. My invitations to Friday night dinner also stopped as food became increasingly scarce because of the war.

Before this, though, in the late spring of 1940, I passed my exams and did quite well in chemistry. I was even able to correct my schoolmates' mistakes in Russian. Shoel and I were only unhappy because we didn't have our family with us. We never lost hope that we would be together again.

Ridder had a very good restaurant where a jazz band entertained every night. We used to drop by to listen – not to eat because we couldn't afford it on our students' allowance. The leader of the band was Jewish and they played mostly American tunes. When we asked the bandleader to play new tunes, he told us that his repertoire was very limited because he hadn't seen any of the new American musicals. Since I loved these movies and had a good ear for memorizing songs, I offered to sing a few of the newer tunes. He wrote down the notes and included these songs in his program. I remembered quite a few songs from musicals written by well-known composers.

The two girls I shared the room with in the dormitory had their boyfriends sleep over quite often. It was called "free love." I found

---

collective farms. The policy met with fierce resistance by peasants and many were persecuted, killed or forcibly resettled in remote regions, especially the more prosperous peasants who were dubbed *kulaks*. For more information, see the glossary.

it very embarrassing, but they were older than me and had no such qualms. Slowly I discovered that they had another character flaw – stealing. The money I received from the school disappeared after I put it under my mattress. The gold ring with my name engraved on it that my parents had given me after I finished school in Lodz was also stolen. I didn't report the losses, nor did I find out for sure who took the items. I just assumed that it had to be one of my roommates.

I, on the other hand, was too honest and never took anything that didn't belong to me, even though there were plenty of opportunities. The school held dances every Sunday night in the gym and one time, in the washroom, someone left a purse on the window sill. I assumed that somebody was in the cubicle, but when I checked, there was nobody there. I took down the purse and saw money and jewellery inside. I could have easily disposed of the purse and kept its contents, but instead I went to the *militsiya* – the civilian police. They thought that I was stupidly naïve to return it and they were right. The purse belonged to one of the teachers and when she got it back, she neither acknowledged nor rewarded me. When she asked me to come to her house, I hoped that I would get something out of it. Instead, she told me to clean the house and never offered me anything to eat or drink. My only reward was honesty.

My life went on pretty much as usual. Every morning we did our exercises outside our rooms for half an hour before going to class. We ate in the cafeteria. One day in the school library I read the newspaper for May 10, 1940, and learned that the Nazis had invaded Holland. Other European countries were falling like dominos. The next day I read that Winston Churchill had become prime minister of England. I passed all my tests and started in the *Tekhnikum's* first year. From now on I was in for a serious education.

My favourite teacher was a homely spinster who taught chemistry and physics. I always sat in front because I liked the subjects very much. I learned what H_2O meant and about atoms and molecules. I was fascinated by the teacher's neatness and couldn't take my eyes off her immaculate white blouse and impossibly clean nails. She lived with her mother and was a very devoted daughter. We called her *Tovarishch*, comrade, and in her classes we behaved well and were treated respectfully.

I also enjoyed the class we took on the French Revolution. We didn't have textbooks, so we had to take notes and be very quick about it or else we wouldn't be able to study for the next lesson.

During one physical education class, when the instructor taught us a new exercise, the language caused me some embarrassment. After he had finished showing us the new exercise, he asked the class, "Zapomnich?" and everybody enthusiastically replied, "Da!"

I was the only one who emphatically shouted, "Nyet!"

In Russian *zapomnich* means to remember, but in Polish it meant the exact opposite – to forget. So when I said, "Nyet," I meant that I would remember. That confusion went on for a few more minutes until I finally understood and said that I would remember. Once we had straightened that out, we had a good laugh and I had learned another Russian word. I didn't make the same mistake again.

The subject I liked least was the study of the Soviet constitution taught by a tall, thin ascetic-looking man who always wore a military tunic, riding breeches and boots. He was incredibly boring, though I never let him know what I thought. He never cracked a smile and was always formal.

The school tried very hard to enroll me in the Young Pioneers movement, which was the Communist Party's children's movement, in order to prepare me for the Komsomol – the youth wing of the Communist Party. The next step would be to become a Communist Party member. I was never enamoured with the concept of communism, but being so young, I couldn't help but be impressed with some people's accomplishments. Aleksei G. Stakhanov, for instance, was famous for being a model Soviet worker who more than fulfilled his quota as a coal miner. People who accomplished similar deeds were awarded the title "Stakhanovietz." I was also impressed by Dolores

Ibaruri who had been the secretary general of the Communist Party in Spain. After the victory of General Francisco Franco and the fascists in the Spanish Civil War, she was considered a heroine of the revolution and found shelter in the Soviet Union. Her words still ring in my ears: "It is better to die on your feet than live on your knees." In my life, I never compromised my principles. That's what these words mean to me. Even though I carried the application form to join the Pioneers for the longest time, I never really considered joining them. I just wasn't interested. I guess I'm a capitalist at heart.

Changing Times

Article 58

My young life started falling apart one beautiful June morning when I was informed that my brother had been arrested, along with five other Jewish men, including Gienia Kaliner's brother Pesach. I had just turned fifteen. I tried to find out what the charges were, but I wasn't able to get any information for months. I was viewed with suspicion and wasn't asked to address the students anymore. I guess my novelty had worn off, even though the students from higher grades still came to me to get help with their textbooks. They had trouble with the Latin script – Russian-language technological books weren't available.

During that same summer of 1940, a young Russian officer named Victor Zagaynov appeared in my life. He was very fond of me and took me out every evening to eat. He always wore a uniform and was quite handsome. We had a good time. He once took me to meet a woman whom he said was his mother. There was a phone in their apartment, which made me very uneasy because no one had private phones. Being so young, I was flattered by his attention and I didn't really give it much thought. It dawned on me much later that perhaps he was sent to gather information about me regarding my brother and the other imprisoned men.

This went on all summer. Victor's behaviour was always at its best until one night he showed up at around midnight and persuaded the night service at the dormitory to call me and the guard let me go with him. We weren't allowed out after ten, but whether he bribed the guard or used his influence as a military man I never found out. Nor did I know what branch of service he was in. He showed up wearing various military uniforms at different times. Against my better judgment I agreed to let him take me for a walk in the park. It was locked at night and the place was empty. Once again, I couldn't figure out how he was able to get into the park. As soon as we got there, he attacked me. It came as a complete surprise because he had always been a perfect gentleman. I suppose if something like this happened now, I might be accused of being an instigator, implying that I had seduced him, that I had no business going out with a man to a deserted park.

My instinct for self-preservation took over and I began fighting him off. I grabbed the cap from his head and tossed it away. That distracted him and while he tried to find it, I seized my chance to escape without being raped. I was prepared to fight like a tigress, ready to die rather than let a rapist deprive me of my virginity at fifteen years of age. The park's gate was locked, but I climbed over the fence into the night, scared and crying. When I returned to the dormitory, I asked the attendant not to let him in again.

I saw him a few more times with a girl on his arm, but I wasn't interested anymore. One experience like that was enough. This girl might have been more willing – or less street smart. A few years later I think I saw him again, but my circumstances then were terrible. I was wearing shabby clothes and boots three sizes too big, and I had lost a great deal of weight due to starvation. We didn't acknowledge each other. Or maybe it wasn't him at all.

When summer came to an end, I still hadn't heard from my brother. School would be starting in September and I had a full year of study ahead of me. By that time I associated mainly with Russian people, or those who spoke Russian. I had very few occasions to speak Yiddish or Polish with anyone.

One day I was called into the principal's office and told to go to the office of the NKVD, the People's Commissariat of Internal Affairs, which later became known as the Committee for State Security or, for short, the KGB.[1] When I arrived, I was taken to a room where an interrogator was sitting behind a red felt-covered desk and another man was taking notes. I was asked to sit down and given a cup of tea. The interrogator began reading the list of charges against my brother. I couldn't believe my ears.

"Shoel Frajlich is accused of crimes under Article No. 58."

I was shocked. Like everyone, I knew what Article 58 was. Punishable by death, imprisonment or hard labour, it applied to anyone deemed guilty of being an "enemy of the workers," of "group agitation and propaganda," or who "...put up resistance to the Red Army."[2]

"Your brother is a traitor," the man said. "He admitted that he was going to buy a gun to kill Stalin." As if getting close to that tyrant was possible. Shoel was also accused of having been in Palestine; the interrogator said that he knew fluent English and was spying for the British.

"These are all lies," I said.

The interrogator showed me papers with my brother's signature on them, but I told them that this was absolutely impossible. Shoel had never been out of Poland, nor did he know a word of English.

The interrogators had a certain flair. They flattered me to try to gain my trust and then accused me of lying and threatened me with

---

1 The NKVD, and later the KGB, functioned as the secret police in the USSR. The organization was known for its cunning and brutality in persuading or intimidating people into giving evidence against or spying on friends and family. For more information, see the glossary.

2 Article 58 of the Soviet Union's Penal Code was brought into force by Stalin in 1928 and was widely applied by the Soviet secret police as a political and arbitrary weapon to arrest, imprison or kill anyone deemed suspicious. For more information, see the glossary.

imprisonment. They meticulously recorded my testimony on paper and then made me sign my name on each page.

This went on for hours. They treated me to a good dinner, then interrogated me some more. They must have thought that softening me up would make me change my story. I had nothing more to add. They showed me pictures that they had taken from my brother the night he was arrested, showing him amidst a group of young people smiling, glasses of beer in their hands. It was just a bunch of people having a good time, all on the threshold of life.

"You see? Your brother is a capitalist," they said, pointing accusingly at the picture.

The interrogation seemed endless. But with the truth on my side, I outlasted them all. Unfortunately, the same wasn't true for my poor brother. Finally they read out his sentence: eight years of hard labour, the standard term for Article 58. I realized that this had been decided even before I was called in for questioning.

"Where is he?" I asked them.

"He is still in the building," they said.

"Can I see him?"

"No."

And that was that. They wouldn't let me see him, if he was there at all. Saying that he was could have been a ploy.

I wasn't called in again to answer their pack of lies. A few months later, I received a letter with no return address and its contents shocked me to the core. It had been smuggled out of the labour camp by a Russian woman who wasn't an inmate but who worked there and had taken pity on my brother. I later found out that she was Jewish. The woman had taken a serious risk in mailing the letter. I had received other letters from Shoel once he was in the labour camp, but they had all been heavily censored. I was surprised that the Russians could read them because the letters were all written in Polish. In this one uncensored letter from my brother, he described very vividly how mercilessly he had been tortured during interrogation, apparently while I was being wined and dined – though, of course, Shoel didn't know that.

"They forced me to sit on one leg of an overturned chair," Shoel wrote. "They shone a blinding light in my eyes and interrogated me." He wrote of more cruelties. When he was finally taken back to his cell, they waited until he was falling asleep and then woke him up to repeat the torture. It is no wonder he signed a confession. He wasn't a very strong person and his tormentors took full advantage of him. The Soviets saved me from the Nazis by allowing me to stay in their country, but what happened to Shoel is something I can neither forgive nor forget.

My brother asked me to send a letter to Mikhail Ivanovich Kalinin, the president of the Supreme Court of the Soviet Union, describing the torture he had suffered from his tormentors. I did as I was asked. Shortly afterward, I received a letter telling me that Shoel's case had been transferred to the Republic of Kazakhstan. From there the case was transferred to the municipality of Ridder, where we were living and where he had been arrested. I was summoned to the city court offices where they informed me that Shoel had been sentenced according to Soviet law and that was the end of it.

I will never understand why the authorities didn't make an effort to learn how I got the information. My brother could have gotten his sentence extended by sending me the letter. I could have been arrested and probably tortured as well, and sent to a hard-labour camp. And I hate to think what they would have done to the kind woman who smuggled out the letter. It wouldn't have surprised me if the Soviet authorities accused her of sabotage and called her an "enemy of the people," a very popular label that they liked to pin on people. I had put myself as well as other people in extreme danger by having the nerve to write to the authorities and complain about the conditions and treatment of prisoners. But besides the formal letters, there was no other reaction. They probably had other things to worry about.

Throughout the second half of 1940 and the first half of 1941, I also received letters from our family sent from the Warsaw ghetto. As I've said before, I have no idea how they ended up there, though I do know that before they went or were taken to Warsaw, they went to stay with my uncle Chaim Moshe and his large family in Bolimów, and then to my grandfather, Kalmen Frajlich, in Lowicz. I read that Uncle Yumi had had a nervous breakdown and had been taken to an insane asylum in Lodz. After that, there was no more news about him in the letters that followed.

My mother soon noticed that Shoel had stopped writing and I had to tell her the truth.

"He was arrested and charged with crimes against Stalin under Article 58," I wrote. "It's a sham. He was set up."

"You should hire a lawyer," she wrote back. It was a naïve assumption – I knew better. It wouldn't have changed anything and, even if I had thought it would, where would I find a lawyer?

The winter of 1940 came along and I was very lonely. I occasionally received letters from my brother, but they were so heavily censored that they didn't contain much information.

When we had volunteered to go to the Russian interior, it was supposed to be for only one year. The term was now about to expire and we were given a choice: to get a Soviet passport and go west to the Ukraine or stay on in Siberia as foreign volunteers with work papers. I had no alternative but to stay on and wait for Shoel's release. As it turned out, the people who opted to take the Soviet passports and go to Soviet Ukraine were never seen again. In a few short months war would break out and they would fall victim to the Nazis as they invaded the western part of the USSR. It was a lucky escape for me, but at what price? The Soviet Union was supposed to be a haven for all races, with no discrimination among the people who inhabited the land. Why, then, did official identity documents indicate your nationality? Mine read, *Yivrei* – Jew.

The newspapers informed us of the changes that were taking place in Europe. One country after another was falling to the Germans

without any resistance. It seemed that the only country that had resisted was Poland, only falling after having its capital city reduced
to rubble. All of Europe was being conquered, but we were so far
removed that we felt quite safe. I still had a place to live and food to
eat, but that wouldn't last very long.

A Different and Difficult Turn

I will always remember June 22, 1941. I had passed my exams at the
Tekhnikum and was looking forward to a relaxing summer. The usually empty marketplace was filled with people, and I was there when
martial music suddenly started blaring from the city's loudspeakers,
followed by a shocking announcement:

"Vnimanye, vnimanye!" (Attention, attention!) "Today at four A M,
without any claims having been presented to the Soviet Union, without a declaration of war, German troops have attacked our country,
attacked our borders at many points and bombed our cities Zhitomir,
Kiev, Sebastopol, Kaunas and some others, killing and wounding over
two hundred persons."

The Soviet Union was being attacked by Nazi Germany. We all
stopped to listen in stunned silence as the speech continued. The
amplified voice coming out of the loudspeakers belonged to Foreign
Minister Vyacheslav Mikhailovich Molotov, the man who had put
his signature next to that of the German foreign minister Joachim
von Ribbentrop when their famous pact was signed on August 24,
1939. The peace had lasted less than two years. Molotov concluded
his speech by declaring, "The enemy is going to be beaten. Victory
will be ours."

As soon as the announcement was over, the martial music re-
sumed. Even during the darkest hours of the war, when it seemed that
we were doomed, Molotov's final words, which we would hear many
times in the months to come, gave us hope and we believed him.

When I got back to my room that day, there was a letter from my family. It would be the very last one. They had included a picture of them all with a dedication written in my sister's handwriting that read, "To our dear Chana and Shoel." This picture is now all I have to show that they existed. I treasure it greatly.

From that day on, my life took a different and difficult turn. The easy ride was over. As I had mentioned in my speech on Red Army Day, when we first arrived in Ridder the work week consisted of five days followed by a day off – a rotation that meant our day off was different each week, as my sister Manya had observed back in Poland. Things now changed and we had to work a constant six-day week with Sundays off. One good thing was that the Soviet government now allowed its citizens a patch of land to plant potatoes or other crops. Previously, owning private land had been considered a crime.

But the worst change of all for me was that I was no longer given a scholarship to attend school. Instead, I was put to work in the school's cafeteria. I had to get up at five in the morning to start working by six. My job was to slice loaves of bread by hand. The students would start arriving at seven for their breakfast so that they could make class by eight.

I had to work until noon and my own classes went from two in the afternoon to eight at night. Now that I was moving up into the higher grades, homework became more difficult. After supper I studied until midnight, got a few hours sleep and then went back to work early the next day. There were no Sundays off for us refugees. We still had to "volunteer" wherever they sent us.

This went on until early winter, which in Siberia sometimes arrived in late August or early September. Because I couldn't manage both school and work, I started missing classes. As a result, I was expelled from the dormitory; I wasn't entitled to live there anymore. I was thrown out one night in mid-December 1941, in a raging snowstorm, and had nowhere to go. I had no warm clothing. My by-now-buttonless coat that my father had made for me was held together with a piece of rope and I had outgrown it. The boots that my sister wore on her honeymoon skiing trip were completely worn out – the flapping soles were held together with pieces of wire.

If there was ever a time in my short life when things seemed hopeless, this was it. No place to stay. Alone. Hungry. No warm clothes. Nobody to care whether I lived or died. I was tempted to just sit down on a snowbank and go to sleep painlessly and permanently. But hope eternal kept me from taking this final step – I hadn't yet lived. Instead, I got up and walked to an apartment complex where some of the people we had come to Ridder with were living. Rather than waking my friends I went down to the furnace room where an old man was keeping the fire going. He kindly shared some bread with me and allowed me to stay until the next morning. He was taking quite a chance helping me because the furnace room was restricted. Luckily, nobody caught us.

After I got some sleep, the kind old man gave me another piece of bread and I left. In the early morning I began walking the seven kilometres to the First Region where the single girls from our group of Polish volunteers were still living in the dormitories. Gienia Kaliner greeted me and I could see from her expression that she couldn't believe her eyes at the sight of me. At first, the other girls weren't exactly enthusiastic about my staying in the dorm with them – I was a mess. But after some strong words from Gienia, they graciously accepted me, heated water for my bath, cleaned me up, gave me some of their own castoff clothing and elevated me to a civilized state. Even though we had lived apart for two years, I felt at home here. My friends shared their food, clothing and whatever they could spare with me. Because I wasn't employed I was only entitled to three hundred grams of bread a day, but at least I had a place to stay where I had a sense of belonging, a common language and customs.

Most of my friends worked in construction and in a brick factory that operated only during the warmer months, starting in April. By the time the factory became operational for the season in April 1942 I had gotten a job there. Even after so many years I can still vividly remember all the steps necessary to form a brick from clay. I worked in a barn-like structure with shelves in it; bricks from the press and cutting machine were put onto the shelves in twos and exposed to the air for a few days until they were dry enough to be separated. My job consisted of climbing onto the shelves to do this. After the bricks had dried sufficiently, the next step was to load them onto wagons and take them first to the kiln, where they were baked for twenty-four hours, and then to the railway to be shipped out.

I liked my job because I was able to work without supervision. I started at five in the morning and when my quota was finished I was allowed to go home – sometimes as early as noon. There were only two of us doing this job, with only the bats living in the building as our companions. I felt like a monkey jumping from shelf to shelf. I never was a clock-puncher or a time-watcher – I liked to be free which got me into a lot of trouble. I was young when I went to the Soviet Union, I hadn't gotten the chance to develop traditional work habits or attitudes, this has stayed with me until today. I function more efficiently without someone telling me what to do, either in my personal or professional life.

Our dormitory was on the edge of a forest. I loved to pick flowers and the air was so pure, with no pollution, that it smelled heavenly, particularly after a rain. I was warned to watch out for snakes, although I never encountered any. All around me, the nature was spectacular and unspoiled. There were mountains, forests and the wide expanse of the Irtysh River. Everything looked so peaceful that it was hard to believe that thousands of kilometres away a vicious fight was taking place for the survival of civilization. It didn't touch us at all as we went about our daily lives. We even occasionally took in a movie, but mostly we worked and tried to receive our daily ration of bread.

When the cold weather set in, my job was eliminated, but I still stayed on with the girls. Because so many men had been mobilized, we had to do all kinds of work on Sundays – the authorities called it "volunteering" but we didn't have much choice about it. The work consisted mainly of gathering crops. With the war raging, food was becoming scarce and ration cards were issued.

I had to earn some money since food had also become very expensive, especially bread, which was selling for 350 rubles a kilo on the black market.[3] Once again the skills I had learned at school in Lodz came in handy and I started doing a lot of knitting for people. The wool I used came from camels that were plentiful here since they provided milk for the native Kazakhs. I hated these dirty, spitting animals. They were shorn and the wool was washed and made into yarn on hand-operated spindles; I never learned how to spin yarn. When the wool was still wet, it gave off a stench that was pungent and nauseating. It could really bowl you over. The sweaters I made weren't the best-smelling, but they were warm and I didn't have to wear one.

I also learned to play guitar. I didn't try to make a career out of it, but played well enough that I was asked to join a band of guitar, mandolin and balalaika players, as well as singers. We performed at least once a week on a regular stage in a club. The conductor was a Polish man for whom I knitted a turtleneck pullover. Apparently he didn't mind the smell.

In the fall of 1942, I was offered work at a local trucking garage by an older Russian man who took a shine to me – or maybe it was just pity. In any event, it gave me the opportunity to work near the dormitory. As part of the job, I had to learn to drive and the garage paid for a six-month driving course. In a class of twenty, there were only two girls – myself and Gienia Kaliner. Everyone in the class except me was employed elsewhere during the day and one by one, the students in the driving course started dropping out. But I was determined to get my license. After six months I would have to pass the test to get the learner's permit that would allow me to operate a vehicle with a licensed driver beside me. After that I would have to pass another exam to get my permanent license.

---

3   The ruble is the unit of currency used in the USSR and in Russia today.

There weren't many students left by the time we were ready to take the first exam. Gienia and I had remained, but a day before the test she hit an electric pole, which knocked out the electricity in the entire region. Luckily she wasn't accused of "sabotage" – one of the regime's favourite accusations – but she decided not to take the test. She got her license years later when she was living in Israel. I passed the test in Ridder.

The vehicles we drove were either a one-ton or half-ton truck made by the Zavod Imieni Stalina, which means "factory named after Stalin," that we called a ZIS, or a three-ton truck called a GAS, which was the acronym for the Gorky Automotive Plant. The trucks were unfortunately more often in the garage shop being repaired than on the road. The ones in good working condition were needed for the war effort.

Many nights, instead of going home to sleep, I had to stay and learn about engines. When I got tired I just pulled out a driver's seat and went to sleep. For some reason I was allowed to do that, but wasn't allowed to go home. I once had the misfortune of hitting a snowbank while driving a GAS and I couldn't get it out by myself. Finally, a flour-carrying tractor trailer showed up and helped me out.

Since I was what was referred to as a *stashor*, a learner, I had a co-driver by the name of Rak, a German man from the Volga River region. These *Volksdeutsche* had lived in that area for generations, but when the war broke out, the Soviet authorities were afraid that they would become a fifth column and exiled them to Siberia.[4] They were good-looking, mechanically minded men, and the Russian women whose husbands or loved ones had left to fight the enemy provided

---

4 *Volksdeutsche* was the term used for ethnic Germans living in countries east of Germany. In August 1941 Stalin ordered the immediate relocation of all the Volga Germans to Kazakhstan, Siberia, and other remote areas. More than 800,000 Soviet Germans were deported between August 1941 and March 1942. A fifth column is a group of clandestine supporters who work within a country to further an invading enemy's military and political aims through espionage or sabotage.

them with all comforts. After all, they never knew if their own men were going to be coming home.

All the trucks had been converted to wood-burning engines and were equipped on each side with samovars, metal urns usually used for making tea but here used to hold wood for the engine to burn. It was my job to keep climbing onto the truck to put cubes of wood into these containers. I also had to get the filter from beneath the carriage of the truck and shake out the soot. By the time I was finished, I was covered in black soot, with only the whites of my eyes showing. Thus I kept *Tovarishch* Rak entertained. He was a good man and let me do most of the driving. We often stopped at government-owned fields and stole potatoes, beets or other vegetables, which we put in the samovars to roast. The beets were especially sweet and we used them in place of sugar, which wasn't available. I still remember Rak fondly – unlike others, he didn't make any sexual demands on me.

I worked in the garage from eight in the morning until five in the afternoon. In the evening we were driven in an open truck to Ridder, seven kilometres away, for lessons – we were taught the mechanics of the engine, maintenance, and so on. One bitterly cold evening, after we got to class, our instructor disappeared. After a long wait, we decided to go to the restaurant he patronized and, sure enough, there he was with his lady friend. He was wining and dining her while we were cold and hungry. He wasn't ready to leave yet and told us to go to the highway and wait for him to take us home. It was close to midnight and freezing outside and I wasn't dressed properly. As a result of the cold, I suddenly had to obey the call of nature. By the time I was finished the rest of the group had left, not realizing that I had been left behind. They didn't even think of taking a head count.

There wasn't a soul anywhere and the howling wind made the electric lines emit strange and frightening sounds. Nothing would be moving on the highway until six the next morning and I was afraid to walk in case I got tired and was tempted to sit down to rest on a snow bank. It would be so easy to fall asleep and never wake up. Instead, I decided to find a place in the hallway of one of the apartment buildings where some of my friends lived. I didn't want to wake them up, so instead tried a few doors until I found one that wasn't locked.

I made myself comfortable in a corner of the hallway to wait until morning when I knew I'd be able to get a ride home by truck. The drivers all knew me from the garage where I worked. But as the old Yiddish proverb goes, "Sleep is a thief." Sure enough, it snuck up on me and I was just starting to fall asleep when all of a sudden, as I was moving to make myself comfortable, a shelf above me started to shake and things started falling down on me. Immediately, a door on my left opened and a man appeared holding a gun in one hand and holding up his pants with the other.

"Get in," he growled, motioning to his apartment. In a panic I did as he ordered and then noticed that he wasn't alone. There was a girl in bed and she was clearly annoyed by my presence.

"Are you a spy?" the man asked in an accusatory tone. "You know, *you* are to blame for the Soviets losing the war." I was curious as to what he meant by "you" but decided not to ask.

"Let me see your documents!" he demanded. I didn't have any identity papers on me, which was a big mistake. In the Soviet Union you never knew when someone was going to stop you and ask you this question. I told him that my papers were in the garage where I worked and tried very hard to convince him that I was telling him the truth. He still didn't believe me and stood there with the gun trained on me the whole time.

All of a sudden a sense of calm came over me and I wasn't afraid. My eyes were glued to the table where there was so much food I couldn't believe what I was seeing. There was bread, herring, salami and other foods I hadn't seen in a very long time. And, of course, there was vodka. I was very hungry and my mouth was watering. All I could see was the food and my inquisitor noticed my hungry stare.

"Sit down. Eat," he said, which further served to annoy his girl-friend. He poured vodka into a glass and told me to drink up. He got angry when I refused the alcohol and insisted that I do as I was told. Then he made me a plate of sandwiches and told me to eat. I gladly obeyed. After I finished eating, he gave me thirty rubles and a red *chervonetz* (gold coin) worth a few more rubles.

"Now, fuck off!" he said.

I lunged at the table, grabbed another piece of bread and then ran out as quickly as I could. It was still night time, but I decided to walk home – after all, I was fortified with food and drink. Fortunately, the last truck carrying coal to the brick factory near my dormitory came along and the driver recognized me and gave me a lift. I never gave a thought to being picked up at night. I climbed on top of the pile of coal and when I got home I didn't even bother to wash up. I went straight to sleep. When I woke up the next morning, I was black and sooty, and still had a piece of bread in my mouth from the night before.

That person who at first seemed to be a fire-breathing dragon of a man turned out to be a sweetheart of a Russian. Even now, I can't help comparing the action of the rabid German soldier at the border tearing my twenty-zloty note in half and putting it into his pocket with the action of this Russian man who started off accusing me of espionage but then showed so much compassion and gave me food and money.

Shoel Ha'cohen

The deterioration of my dear, sweet brother and how I handled it will always be the most painful chapter of my life. It is something I will never get over.

One morning in the autumn of 1942 I came back to the dorm after working the night shift and found my brother, Shoel, sitting on the stairs. He had been there all night in the bitter cold because one of the girls, Eva Goldberg, was afraid of contracting his tuberculosis and had thrown him out. This picture will stay with me until my dying day. Eva is dead now, but I can neither forgive her nor forget what she did. She may well have hastened his death. I find it extremely difficult to write about it even now.

Shoel had been released from the hard-labour camp after two and a half years thanks to Polish General Wladyslaw Anders, who helped negotiate the amnesty of thousands of imprisoned Polish citizens.[5] The goal was to recruit a Polish army to fight alongside the Soviets, but by the time he was released, Shoel was too sick to sign up.

I couldn't believe it was the same Shoel. The beautiful winter coat that had been new when we left Poland and fitted him so well now hung loosely on his wasted body. His blue eyes were sunken in their sockets. He had endured such horrific, inhuman torture. At the time I didn't realize how sick he was and that there was no known cure for tuberculosis. The disease wasn't just in his lungs, his whole body was consumed. He stayed with me in the dorm room I shared with the other girls – he had no other place to stay. I shared my food with him and even used the same utensils although he was coughing up blood. I could easily have become infected with the disease myself, but I didn't think about it at all.

I suspected all along that one man from our group of refugees, a Warsawer named Yaakov Kolber, had been the one to denounce Shoel and the others who had been falsely charged and sentenced to hard labour. Like many other Polish Jewish refugees, he had been a member of the Jewish Workers' Alliance of Lithuania, Poland and Russia that was known by its Yiddish acronym, the Bund.[6] Some of

---

5 General Anders was the Polish army officer who formed and led a large force of Polish exiles in the Soviet Union after June 1941. Many of the men who joined Anders had been prisoners who were released from Soviet labour camps and prisons expressly for this purpose. Initially intended to fight alongside the Red Army, the so-called Anders Army left Soviet territory in 1942 through Iraq, Iran and Palestine, and eventually formed the bulk of the Second Polish Corps that fought in Italy. For more information, see the glossary.

6 The Bund was a Jewish social-democratic revolutionary movement founded in 1897 that fought for the rights of the Yiddish-speaking Jewish worker in Eastern Europe and Russia and was especially active in Poland and Lithuania. For more information, see the glossary.

the people in our group and their families had been Bundists before the war – not ours, though. My parents were staunch believers in capitalism and were heartbroken when Manya had had her brief fling with communism. I suspected that Kolber must have been threatened by the NKVD to either rat on the "traitors" from his group – that is, those who weren't avowed Communists – or face imprisonment or even death. In order to save his own skin, he named names and thus contributed to the arrest of innocent people.

Others had been arrested along with Shoel, including Pesach, Gienia Kaliner's brother. At the time Gienia had vowed, "May whoever is guilty of betraying them have his tongue cut out of his head!" Much later in the war, when both Pesach and Kolber were fighting with the Soviet army as it moved west into Poland, a Soviet Army notice arrived addressed to Kolber's girlfriend, Gienia Meyersdorf. The letter informed her that Kolber had been shot in the throat in a battle at the front and the bullet couldn't be removed because it was close to the artery and taking it out would mean certain death. Kolber's wound became gangrenous and the doctors had to remove his tongue. He died of typhus. When Eva Goldberg heard this, she said to Gienia, "Look what you've done! You cursed him!"

Soon after he arrived at our dorm, Shoel had to be admitted to the hospital in Ridder. When this happened I came down with another case of wanderlust: I decided to leave the dorm and my job at the garage and follow him to the city.

By late fall in 1942, Shoel was in and out of hospital and food was very scarce. Things were going very badly for the Soviets at this point in the war and every effort had to be made to support the Red Army.[7]

---

7 From July to November 1942, the Red Army was mired in the Battle of Stalingrad in what became the bloodiest battle in modern history – with an estimated total of 2 million casualties from both sides. By early 1943 a Soviet counter-offensive was underway that eventually led to the defeat of the German army at Stalingrad in early February 1943 and to a turning point in the war in favour of Allied forces.

It was quite common for me to go without food for two or three days at a time. I now had no fixed place to live, no change of clothing. The state of my hygiene, after not having a bath all winter, I will leave to your imagination. As soon as some of the ice thawed, the Irtysh River became my bathtub. On its shores I stripped and washed the lice out of my rags.

When spring arrived I went into the fields and started digging for potatoes left from the fall harvest. What I found were empty potato skins containing some very dry starch. Even that was good enough. I added some water, made pancake batter and cooked it on top of the stove. I couldn't even add salt because it was rationed and I didn't have any. The results were so awful that I became violently ill after eating them. It wasn't even suitable for a pig. In fact, I'm sure pigs had better food. At that time I considered myself lucky if I was able to get a piece of *makucha*, a sunflower-oil cake that was made from the crushed shells of sunflower seeds after most of the oil had been pressed out. It was used to feed livestock but one piece of *makucha* could last me a whole day because it was so hard to chew. It really wasn't meant for human consumption, but I couldn't be choosy. At least it kept my stomach juices flowing.

My young age and inexperience made it difficult for me to cope with life's hardships. But considering the fate of my family and that of other Jews, I was more than lucky. My only dream was to be re-united with my family. None of us could yet grasp the full extent of our tragedy.

The last time Shoel was admitted to hospital was sometime in February 1943. We were in the same city, but I couldn't help him much. I had found a job in the mine's cafeteria washing dishes in a huge copper vat. Miners worked two shifts of twelve hours each – there were thousands of bowls.

When my brother left for the hospital that last time, he was so weak that he fell down some steps. Why did I not help him? I cannot erase this picture from my mind. It has haunted me forever. Didn't I see how sick he was? He had so many unlived years ahead of him. He was only twenty-three years old, a victim of both the Nazis and the Soviet regime, thanks to a fellow member of our own tribe.

At least my work provided me with some food, mostly just soup – the meat was reserved for the miners. Between my shifts of doing dishes, I was assigned to peel potatoes. They were actually peeled by machine, but the water to wash the potatoes had to be brought in from the river just outside the door. There were no sewer outlets inside, so I also had to empty the peeling machine's buckets outside. It was a back-breaking and dangerous job, and I kept slipping and sliding in the severe Siberian winter. It was only by sheer luck that I didn't fall and break any bones.

I would work a twenty-four-hour shift and then have forty-eight hours free. During that time, I went to see my brother. One time, in the middle of a conversation, he fell silent and closed his eyes. His eyelids were translucent. I panicked, but he opened his eyes and said, "I'm not dead yet."

On my last visit, Shoel shared with me his only last wishes: "I want to go home, have a piece of white bread and butter, a glass of tea with lemon, kiss our mother goodbye and die." Just before I left, he asked me to take his clothes with me, along with some money.

"No, Shoel," I said, "I'll come back after my next shift. I'll pick up your things then." There was no phone I could use to inquire about him and, of course, I couldn't take time off to see him in the middle of my shift.

On Thursday, March 18, 1943, when my shift was over and I was ready to go to the hospital, a messenger came with the news that Shoel had passed away a few hours earlier. When I got to the hospital, a nurse told me that his last words were, "Is my sister here?" I wasn't there when he took his last breath and those painful words would always ring in my ears. Shoel died alone.

With my last connection gone, I became an orphan. Despite the things he had wished for on his deathbed, all Shoel got was a lonely death. There was no piece of bread and butter, no glass of tea with lemon. Nor did he get to kiss our dear mother, whose fate we didn't know.

A few days before Shoel died, I had had a disturbing dream:

I am walking up a dark, wooden staircase, hanging onto the shaky wooden banister for dear life. When I reach the third floor, I take off a key that hangs from an oval ring. I open the door and let myself in. The kitchen is in semi-darkness, lit only by the light from the next room. I enter and what I see, or what I assume I see, is my family, sitting around a table covered with a white tablecloth. Our silver candlesticks are on the table, one still slightly bent, the candles are shining bright ... food is on the table. I realize that it must be Friday night – the Sabbath. I can only see my mother clearly. The others are just shadows.

As I stand in the doorway, my mother says, "Come in. Why are you standing there? Sit down and eat." I remain standing.

"Where is my son, Shoel?" she asks.

"He'll be here soon," I reply.

My mother's face becomes very sad and very quietly, through tears, she says, "No, he will never come back!" Her mournful crying breaks my heart.

When I awoke from the dream, my face was wet with tears that I couldn't stop. I knew she was right. I knew the meaning of my dream, no matter how hard I tried to reject the interpretation.

I couldn't make myself view Shoel's body, never having seen a corpse before. That is another thing for which I will never forgive myself until my dying day.

At the hospital, the vultures had descended – the things my brother wanted me to take home had disappeared before I got there. It didn't matter to me anyway. I had lost the last connection to my family – the last link was gone. I was desperately alone, lonely and poor. Nobody offered to help arrange his burial and I took three days off from work without permission to do it but without success. Eventually this decision to leave work would land me in a hard-labour camp for six months and in the end it had to be left to the city to look after Shoel's burial. Ten days after his death, during a very heavy snowfall, my married friend Hela Picksman allowed me to stand in the window of her apartment and watch the sled carrying my brother's body to the cemetery where he was buried in an unmarked grave.

The fact that Shoel wasn't buried in accordance with Jewish law, which proscribes burial within twenty-four hours and a mourning period of seven days, is another load of guilt that I carry. Like my father, Shoel was a *cohen*, a noble descendant of the Jewish high priests of the Temple, worthy of the highest burial rites. I couldn't go with him for his final sendoff. I had no shoes or warm clothes. I silently said my goodbye when the sled disappeared from view. Hela interrupted the saddest moment of my life by asking me to leave her home because she didn't want her husband to find me there. She made me feel like a leper. I was a sorry sight and not a very clean one.

I knew that Shoel had left some things with a Jewish family with whom he had stayed for awhile. When I went to claim my brother's belongings, they refused to turn them over to me. Instead, they accused me of theft. I had no choice but to take them to court. The woman, a single mother from Warsaw, was very smart and I was no match for her. Even the police couldn't do anything – there were rumours that she was bribing them with sex. She didn't even show up on the day of the court hearing. The police had to be dispatched to get her. She lost the case, but all that was recovered was a white skirt – probably her own – and a bar of soap.

It has been many years since the day Shoel died. But the grief and guilt is as raw as ever. If anything, I think about him even more often now. At least I know when to light the *yahrzeit* candle in his memory – the eleventh day of Adar ii, 5703.[8] He is the only member of my family whose date of death and approximate place of burial I know.

---

8 *Yahrzeit* is observed on the anniversary of the relative's death according to the Jewish calendar. For more information, see the glossary.

Alone

Progul

How I survived six months following Shoel's death in March 1943 can only be called miraculous. The group I arrived in the Soviet Union with in early 1940 had stayed closely together, but I had been separated from them when the authorities put me in school. I was only fourteen years old at the time and I hadn't been able to develop close attachments to this community – my circumstances had put me outside the group's protective shield. To put it bluntly, I was a misfit and an outsider. I didn't know where I belonged. And now, I had nowhere to sleep and no one to look after my wellbeing.

When Shoel was arrested and I was interrogated by the N K V D, the Soviet authorities had confiscated all our documents from Poland. I never got anything back and I no longer had anything to prove who I was or how old I was. When I applied for the job in the mine cafeteria they had sent me to a doctor to determine my age. After looking inside my mouth and checking my teeth like a horse, the doctor determined that I was nineteen instead of seventeen, that I was born in 1923, not in 1925. Because I was going to work with food in the commissary, they also performed the necessary medical screening tests and one showed that I had parasites in my stool. I was admitted to hospital for three days. The choice was either go to the hospital for treatment or not be allowed to handle food and thus lose my job and income. While I was there, a young woman with laboured and raspy breathing was brought into my room and put in the bed next to mine. It was awful. At some point I became aware that I no longer heard her breathing, and knew that she had died. None of the medical staff realized what had happened, so I got out of bed and paced the corridor until they took her body away.

Immediately after Shoel died, I walked off the job at the mine's cafeteria so I could make funeral arrangements. This was against the law and was a very serious offence, especially during the war. I didn't think about the consequences – those would emerge later. The crime of being absent from work without permission was called *progul* and for that crime I was sentenced to six months imprisonment in a hard-labour camp. Before the authorities could arrest me, however, they had to find me. Soon after Shoel died I found another job in a *poly-clinic*, a medical clinic, cleaning and sterilizing surgical instruments. But when they tried to teach me to give injections to patients, I left. I couldn't stand the sight of blood. Again, I got itchy feet. I was what they called *brodiaga*, a hobo, without a steady place to live. I mention this because one result of all my moving around was that the police didn't know how to find me when they wanted to arrest me for the crime of being absent from work.

I did a lot of odd jobs during that summer. I helped people look after their small patches of land where they planted whatever they could – mostly potatoes. The soil was very fertile for this crop and they were able to grow enormous potatoes. The small plots of land also produced an abundance of beets, tomatoes, cucumbers and other vegetables. It was hard work and we had to hurry to harvest the crops before the cold weather set in and the crops froze. Most people gave me pails full of potatoes for my work, but one of the peasant families had a cow (that was all they were allowed to own by Soviet law) and they paid me with milk. I often traded the milk for potatoes, which really helped because now that I was no longer formally employed, I didn't have a bread ration card.

One day I was just walking on the outskirts of town, surrounded by fields of ripe red tomatoes, yellow honeydew melons and potatoes waiting to be picked. People were working all around me and I suddenly heard a conversation in what I thought was Polish. I found it quite difficult to follow since the dialect was so different from the one that we spoke in central Poland. The speakers turned out to be a family consisting of elderly parents, their daughter and her two school-age children from Vilna. They had been allocated quite a large plot of land and were finding it difficult to work it themselves. They allowed me to stay with them in their mud cabin for the duration of the season. We shared meals, but questions were never asked. My job was simply to dig potatoes from underneath huge bushes. One person had to dig from one end while the other stood on the other side pulling. The potatoes were enormous. I'd never seen anything like it. We also gathered beets and onions that had been planted between the potato bushes.

Religion never came up in conversation. When they went to prayers on Sunday, they didn't ask me to come along. Like the saying goes, "Ask me no questions and I'll tell you no lies." I enjoyed this family's company and we parted as good friends at the end of the picking season. I don't even remember if I got paid – it wasn't terribly important to me.

The warmer weather enabled me to cleanse myself of the dirt and whatever other unsavory things my body had accumulated. I sat on the bank of the Irtysh River, and stripped off my dirty clothes and allowed the water to purify me. It was also warm enough for me to sleep outside. My bed was the ground; moss my mattress; leaves my pillow. The girls at the dormitory shared their own meagre rations with me whenever I showed up on their doorstep.

Other members of our group had had their own share of misfortune. Gienia Kaliner's brother, Pesach, had also been falsely accused, imprisoned and then released with Shoel. He married another member of our group, Tamara, who was considerably older than he was.

They had a baby boy who died after only a few months. After he was freed, Pesach had found employment in a flour mill, but was arrested again for trying to take home a couple of kilos of flour for his family. He was given two choices: either go to jail or join the Red Army and fight the Germans on the Polish front. He chose the second option and left for the front with the dubious Yaakov Kolber and another member of our group, Abie Naihaus.

While Pesach was moving westward through Europe with the Red Army in 1944, he began to look for family members. He wrote back to Gienia, "There is nothing left – not a single stone remains, let alone a single person. There is nothing but silence and rubble everywhere." He searched all the surrounding towns and found much of the same everywhere he went. Sensing that the war would soon be over, he wrote another letter telling of his plans to come back to Ridder. That was the summer of 1944. He was never heard from again. In that way, Gienia and I shared a similar fate. Both of us arrived with brothers, only to leave alone and go home to nothing and nobody.

But before this, as the summer of 1943 came to an end, so did my escapades. Five months after Shoel's death, at the end of August 1943, I went to see one of the girls in our group, Gucia, to see if I could spend the night at her place. Gucia was Tamara's sister, though the two sisters had become estranged. Gucia lived alone in a one-room apartment, which was very unusual because most of us had to share accommodations. I should have been suspicious that she had a place to herself. At any rate, she let me stay with her overnight. My intention was to spend the next day picking some of the wild blueberries that grew in abundance on the mountain. I hoped to sell them to make a few rubles so that I could buy a loaf of black-market bread, which cost 350 rubles a kilo. I was in a very difficult position – I couldn't find work because I had no steady address and therefore all I was entitled to was 300 grams of bread a day. As far as the authorities were concerned, I was a parasite, of no use or benefit to anyone.

I got up very early the next morning, careful not to wake up

Gucia, and let myself out. My young legs had no problem getting me to the top of the mountain and I started picking. At first the berries kept falling through the cracks in the baskets' weave, but I solved that problem by lining them with leaves. By late afternoon I had two baskets full of berries. Along with other pickers, I started back down the mountain, carefully walking down along the winding path. The previous night's rain had made it very slippery and I was barefoot. I gripped the pebbles with my toes to avoid sliding. Other more agile pickers ran past me, eager to get their merchandise to market. All I cared about was getting down safely. I was almost halfway down when I dared to look below and saw a lot of commotion at the bottom – a van, a police car and people waiting to see who they were going to nab.

I made it down safely, but was immediately taken into custody. Without asking me my name, the authorities already knew exactly who I was. As soon as we got to the police station, I was taken to a room where the charges and my sentence were read aloud. I was accused of *progul*, absenteeism. I was considered a criminal because I hadn't shown up for work for several days. I was also guilty of escaping custody after my brother had passed away. My crime of *progul* had actually only earned me a three-month sentence in a hard-labour camp, but – if you can believe it – because I had no permanent address and they hadn't been able to find me my sentence had been doubled to six months. I had been tried in absentia and found guilty. Along with other similar "criminals," I was going to be taken to a camp some 120 kilometres away. I had nothing but the clothes on my back.

I paid dearly for Gucia's so-called hospitality – I can only assume that she was the one who denounced me to the NKVD. She clearly had connections and was the only one who knew that they were looking for me.

Years later, during one of my visits to Israel, I found out that Gucia, her only son, her daughter-in-law and their baby had all come to a very tragic end. The young couple and their baby had been killed in a car accident and Gucia was found a few days later in her apartment, dead of natural causes. Do I feel that justice was done as far as she was concerned? Not at all. Nobody deserves to die alone like that. She is gone, but I am still around to write about it and I can't help but feel sorry for the kind of person she was.

Gucia's sister Tamara, who became Gienia Kaliner's sister-in-law, was always around when I was starving and fed me bowls of soup and pieces of bread. I will always remember how she was still able to be kind despite the loss of her husband, Pesach, and her baby.

Hard Labour

I began my labour sentence in early September 1943. Before we set out for the work camp near Ust-Kamenogorsk,[1] the other prisoners' families came to see them off and give them food. I could only look on wistfully with an empty stomach. All the way to our destination I kept wondering who might have denounced me. Although I had my suspicions, I had no proof.

The work camp where I served out my sentence was relatively small with just a few barracks, one of which was for Finnish prisoners of the Soviet-Finnish War of 1939.[2] They were kept almost completely separate from other prisoners. I don't remember seeing them performing any labour and I didn't even see them at mealtime. There was a *bolnitza*, or clinic, a dining room and a kitchen. The camp was

---

1 Located on the Irtysh River, 120 kilometres southeast of Ridder and 3,000 kilometres from Moscow, Ust-Kemenogorsk is a major mining and metallurgical centre and important transporation junction. It is known as Oskemen in Kazakh.

2 Also called the Winter War, the Soviet-Finnish War began on November 30, 1939, when the Soviets attacked Finland, which had been attributed to its "sphere of influence" in the Molotov-Ribbentrop Pact. The war lasted until March 12, 1940, when the Finns conceded. Approximately 3,500 Finnish prisoners of war were held in Soviet camps. For more information, see the glossary.

run almost exclusively by the *zakliuchonye*, or prisoners, but the real power resided with the *volnye*, or free citizens. These were people who had served out most of their sentence and had been released for good behaviour but who continued to live at or near the camp. They weren't technically prisoners anymore, but were almost more like colonists.

When we arrived, we were processed, assigned to work on building a railroad and issued clothes and *traktory*, heavy shoes made from recycled tires that were worn without socks. Our brigade consisted of twenty young people, only three of whom were women. The next day we were taken out by train to work on extending the narrow local railway line. The wakeup call was at five o'clock in the morning and before we set out to work we got a meal consisting of soup, bread and tea. We were counted and then escorted out of the gate by some aged guards armed with ancient rifles. A small train swiftly took us downhill to the work site. Sparks from the train's wood-fired engine flew all around us and we all walked around in coats full of charred holes. I was assigned to carry the heavy rails with another girl and turn them over to the men. The third girl, who was the foreman's favourite, did the cooking. We didn't go to the camp for meals since it took the train much longer to get back up the hill, but at least we were given more soup, bread and tea.

Most of the barracks weren't locked at night so that we could use the outhouse and our movements inside the camp weren't restricted. But outside the gates, we were under the supposedly watchful eye of a *strelok*, or sharpshooter. In reality an old guard just sat there with a rickety rifle between his knees. He was bored and would sometimes fall asleep. We would amuse ourselves by waking him up to ask him if we could relieve ourselves. He didn't seem terribly interested in following or checking our whereabouts. Whenever I saw him reach for his tobacco pouch, I would approach him and ask for a smoke. He almost never refused and even taught me how to roll my own *papiros* – cigarettes. Most of what he had was *machorka*, a type of homegrown tobacco. For the most part, the guards were decent men who had been called up to replace the young men who were needed to fight the Nazis.

A work day at the camp came to a close after fourteen long hours. Back at the camp, we were given another meal that consisted of a salty, bitter fish soup called *ucha*. It was inedible. Some of the prisoners ate as much of the fish, including the bones, as they could. They would get so thirsty and drink so much water that they would swell up and the authorities would release them because they didn't want to risk any fatalities on their watch. I remember one young man named Ivan Petrov who got himself released this way. He was only in his early twenties and was very anxious to be freed. I think that if he hadn't been successful, he would have ended up being buried in the camp cemetery. On reflection, when I think of the poor victims of the concentration camps, we were well looked after in comparison. We weren't singled out because we were Jews.

When the weather turned cold and snowy, we couldn't work on laying the rails. Instead, we were given wooden shovels to clear the road near the camp so that food and supplies could be brought in. Sometimes the snowbanks were so high that they hid the electric poles. When that happened, we were sent to cut down trees on the mountain with manual handsaws to provide wood for heating the barracks. It took two people to perform this work and my partner was an older Russian man. I became very proficient in judging which tree was going to fall from its tilt. When the tree fell, it would get buried in the snow and we had to clear around it. Next, we would cut it into logs half a metre long and then chop the pieces into firewood. The trees were very moist and only needed to be hit with an axe at a certain angle to split. There were usually horses and sleds to take the firewood to camp, but whenever there was a severe snowstorm, the horses were kept in the stables and the prisoners had to do it. We would form a chain along the mountain and hand the logs from top to bottom until each had reached its destination.

I soon developed a severe infection and was in terrible pain from the constant rubbing of the *traktory* against my unprotected feet. I couldn't take it any longer, so one morning I decided to take matters into my own hands and didn't leave the camp for work. After all, I thought, what could they do, arrest me? After everybody had left, though, an inspection team showed up to see what had happened to the absent prisoner. One of the team members, another prisoner, grabbed me and threw me down from the upper bunk where I slept. Still, I refused to go to work. I could have been given an extension of my sentence or even been accused of sabotage, but I stood my ground and insisted that they let me see a doctor. Fortunately for me, the doctor was a Jewish woman, an evacuee from Kiev,[3] She looked at my ankle, applied some ointment and released me from joining my work detail. The doctor authorized the camp management to give me some lighter work, however, because doing nothing would have meant not being allowed to eat. I was put up on a scaffold with a pail of white-wash and a brush and told to start painting. But the scaffolding collapsed and I fell to the ground, twisting my ankle. At that point, the doctor released me from work for the entire day.

A very serious and dangerous problem arose that same day. Another girl had also booked off sick, but she wasn't too sick to rummage through all of the packages that the prisoners had received from their families on visiting day. The contents were mostly home-baked bread, slabs of bacon and salted lard. I was salivating – the smell of the food was overpowering. I didn't care if it was pork as long as it would fill my stomach – I'd observe *kashruth* later. The girls sometimes shared their food with the other prisoners, but I would never

---

3 After the German attack and invasion of 1941, over a million Soviet citizens, especially skilled workers, were evacuated from the major cities in the western part of the country – such as Kiev, Leningrad and Moscow – and relocated beyond the Ural Mountains. The Soviet government also moved thousands of factories to safety in this way.

have dared to help myself – my fellow prisoners weren't just petty criminals like me; some of them were murderers. Not wanting to be a witness to her activities, I turned my face to the wall and pretended to be asleep.

When the work gang returned and discovered that somebody had gone through their things, all hell broke loose. One prisoner who had been sentenced to eight years for murdering her mother-in-law ordered the rest of us to close the only door to the barracks. Somehow, I was never suspected, but she soon found the guilty party and punished the culprit mercilessly, almost beating the life out of her. For the first time in my life I saw how vicious women can be. When I later heard the stories of women guards in the concentration camps, I had no trouble believing them. After almost killing the thief, the murderess told us, "Outside this camp you can do whatever your conscience dictates. But here, we're all equal. There are no special privileges." I wasn't sure if this was some kind of honour code among thieves, but we all listened. When we were called out to the camp's office one at a time later in the evening, all of a sudden, we were all deaf, dumb and blind.

I was personally interrogated by Mr. Zalcman, the aide to the camp's *nachalnik* (director). Zalcman was also a prisoner and Jewish; although he didn't admit it, his name and thick Jewish accent betrayed him and I wasn't fooled. He was serving eight years for being a *spekulant* – a speculator – a title he earned by selling rice on the black market. In the Soviet system, rice or anything supposedly sold for profit, had the same value as a human life, as my poor, dear brother's death showed. One old man I knew received a two-year sentence for stealing a spoon from a government cafeteria. He didn't survive and was buried outside the camp.

When Mr. Zalcman questioned me, I denied seeing or hearing anything. He tried to bribe me with a kitchen job, but I kept to my story out of fear. I was sure that we both knew the truth and I worried that from now on he was going to take out his frustrations on me, but that isn't what happened. Instead, he gave me an evening job peeling potatoes in preparation for the next day's meals. I didn't mind, but because I was so near food while I was working, I overate and was stricken with the runs until my stomach adjusted. The food I ate was cow intestine, which is called tripe in polite company. In a way I felt that Mr. Zalcman admired me for sticking to my story. My only fear was that the guilty one might suspect that I had snitched. Otherwise, why would I be chosen for this job? But there were no further complications from the incident.

January 1944 arrived and although the days were very short, we didn't get reduced hours at work. It was unbelievably cold. When the sun disappeared, hidden by the mountains, so did whatever warmth it gave. But, oh, the scenery – the mountains, the rivers and the forests! The trees stood tall and straight, almost reaching the sky. It was majestic in all its splendour. It was almost impossible to believe that such beauty could exist side-by-side with such misery.

The old man who was my work partner told me a lot about his family and I told him about mine as we spent hours cutting down the trees in the forest. Our release dates were approaching and he invited me to meet his family after I got out. I intended to take him up on his offer, but due to many circumstances, it took me awhile to make it to his home. Unfortunately, he wasn't there – he had never made it home and nobody knew what had happened to him. In Siberia people just disappeared. He may have been killed for the few rubles he would have been carrying, or perhaps he froze to death on his way home. I never went back to find out.

As my release date got closer, I developed serious health problems. My body was breaking down thanks to an iron deficiency and I developed *kurinaya slepota*, which literally means hen's blindness, but we know it as night blindness. I couldn't see at all in the dark and had to hang on to somebody to guide me. Fortunately, the condition was short-lived – it was alleviated by the longer days. I was looking forward to my release but also feared my freedom. Where would I go? What would my future be?

Then two weeks before my release and transfer to a much larger camp for processing, I developed a high fever. The doctors suspected typhoid and cut off my hair. I didn't regret saying goodbye to the lice and the nits. The typhoid scare was a false alarm, but a blessing nonetheless. We were supposed to spend our days off at camp delousing each other, but I could never do it, nor did I allow anybody to do it to me.

By now it was the end of February 1944 and for the last two weeks of our sentence we were put to work in the larger camp freeing logs from the ice in the Irtysh River. It was a backbreaking job in extremely cold weather and we didn't have proper clothing. Our felt boots, *valenki*, were soaking wet. When I put mine near the *piechka*, or stove, to dry out, they got holes in them from the sparks. Needless to say, we weren't issued new ones. We just stuffed some paper inside them, which wasn't much help. There were no windows in the barracks in this new camp, just a couple of dim, bare bulbs that stayed lit all night. I didn't spend enough time there to remember much about the surroundings, but I do remember that there were thousands of us.

Freedom Once Again

My day of freedom finally arrived. One day the five o'clock bell still woke us, but I didn't have to get up with the rest of the prisoners. I didn't have to rush – there would be no work for me today. But I did have to get up to go to the mess hall for breakfast. Just as in the other camp, breakfast consisted of a very thin soup, a slice of black bread and something resembling dirty dishwater that they called tea.

At six o'clock all the prisoners lined up according to their group's destination. They marched through the gate escorted by the guards to begin a long day's work. Very excited, I ran to the main office where the list of prisoners to be released was posted. To my chagrin, my name wasn't on it. When I asked why, I was told, "Your name is Frajlich. That's a German name. We have to check if you are a German."

"How long will that take?" I inquired anxiously.

"It may take an hour, a day, or a month," came the answer. The wheels of Soviet bureaucracy could turn very slowly.

I went back to the barracks to await further news. None came until I went to the office again and, to my relief and joy, this time my name was on the list. I was the only one who had been detained and when the bell rang for lunch, I found out that I wasn't entitled to any more food. That was only for the prisoners who were still working. I ended up having to go hungry for the rest of the day, which was nothing new to me. Before my imprisonment I had only eaten every second or third day. The camp really spoiled me – they fed me three times a day!

I was free – or so I thought. They gave me some papers and they may have even given me a small amount of money – I have to admit that I really don't remember. I intended to return to Ridder, back to my so-called home to join my friends. So much had changed in my life since we had all arrived together in 1940. On my way to the gate, though, I realized that I was wearing a sleeveless vest that hadn't been issued to me. I quickly went back to the barracks, took it off and left it there. If I had quite innocently taken it, I would have been searched and accused of stealing government property. I could have faced another term in camp. This was an opportunity I wasn't willing to give them.

My first step to freedom found me wearing a *fufaika*, a quilted prisoner's jacket, next to my naked body. No bra. As a matter of fact, I didn't wear a bra until I was twenty-one years old and back in Poland. I had a string around the jacket's waist and a pair of quilted pants with no underwear. I wore *valenki* and no socks. A quilted hat with patches on top covered my ears and my nearly bald head, still freshly shorn from the typhoid scare. After four years in the Soviet Union that was the sum of my possessions.

The gate opened, I surrendered my release papers to the guards and took my first step toward freedom in six months. It was early afternoon, with brilliant sunshine. The sky was incredibly blue and extremely cold. As I kept walking, every now and then I kept turning around to look at the camp, not believing that I was free. A sled went by with some camp officials. They checked my papers and off they went. Still, I kept turning around, happy that no one was following me to take me back. The land was very flat and the camp kept getting smaller as the distance increased. Finally I could see it no more. I was on my own in Siberia, two thousand kilometres east of the Ural Mountains, five hundred kilometres from China, Mongolia and other Asian countries to the south. I was also six thousand kilometres from home.

When I reached the railroad station in Ust-Kamenogorsk, the train was ready to leave, its engine puffing steam. Unfortunately, as it turned out, I wasn't entitled to board it without a pass from the *militsiya*, the local police. Worse was yet to come. There was only one train a day and that was it! Where was I going to find shelter for the night or food to eat? Where would I wait for the train to take me to my destination the next day? Why the camp officials didn't provide released people with passes is beyond me. I couldn't have predicted this situation. It was just another case of a very cruel system not caring. At least they should have shown some compassion and asked me how I was going to get to wherever I was going.

In desperation, I pretended that I was willing to accept my lot, but when the train started moving, I jumped aboard. The female conductor tried to push me off, but I hung on for dear life and as the train started picking up speed, she had no choice but to pull me inside. A young soldier approached me, looked over at me and said resentfully, "How come somebody as young as you isn't in the army?"

"Do you think I'm a boy?" I replied.

He took a closer look and realized his mistake. It was just my luck that I had boarded this particular coach, which was filled with Red Army soldiers.

"Rebyata!" (Boys!) said the young soldier. "There is a female among us!" The others all crowded around me, curious. I did look more like a boy than a girl. I was surprised that they could tell the difference, although with some difficulty, and I didn't feel that I deserved to be an object of any male admiration, especially with my hair shorn off. The conductor who only a short while ago had tried to push me off the train now came to my rescue and took me to a separate compartment. I was surprised to see that I was going to be in the company of an old man and a kid who was younger than me. Unfortunately, it turned out that we were all under arrest for the crime of boarding the train without passes. Once again, I was under the watch of an armed guard. My freedom had only lasted for three hours.

Arrested Again, Released Again

When we arrived in Ridder we were paraded through the city under guard as three dangerous criminals. What crimes my fellow prisoners had committed I didn't know because we weren't allowed to communicate with each other. I was freezing cold and very hungry. My eyelashes kept icing up from my breath and I had to keep scraping them to be able to see. By now it was late afternoon or rather early evening. The sun disappeared and the temperature dropped still further. When we finally reached the city jail, I was put in a holding cell with other women. At least I could thaw out. My cellmates were only in their underwear and bras, but I kept my clothes on. I didn't want to embarrass myself since I had nothing on underneath.

The guards brought in food and we lined up for our portion of hot soup and bread. The food was much tastier than at the camp, or maybe I was too hungry to care. I ate my food quickly and had lined up for seconds when one of the women suddenly hit me in the face. She said that I'd be entitled to seconds only when I had spent as much time in jail as the others had.

I was glad that it had nothing to do with my being Jewish. Clearly the law of seniority applied here as well. Someone told me quietly that the woman who had hit me in the face was in jail for murder. She was awaiting sentencing and would probably get eight years, the standard punishment. For the rest of the night I sat on the floor, trying to make myself invisible so that I wouldn't antagonize her. She didn't bother me again. I guess she forgot about me.

In the morning I demanded to see the *procurator*, the district attorney. The officials in the jail finally let me go to see him, unescorted. They probably thought that I wasn't a danger to society anymore, even as a repeat offender. The lawyer turned out to be another Jewish evacuee from Kiev – I seemed to be making quite a habit of running into them. He listened to my tale of woe and found it quite amusing – although I couldn't see what was so funny about having to spend the night with hardened criminals – and let me go. On the positive side, at least I got a meal and a warm place to spend the night.

Finally, I really was free to go and join my friends, who lived seven kilometres from Ridder. I had to walk; there weren't any buses. When I reached my destination, everybody was shocked at my appearance and started to clean me up as they had once before. One of them, my beloved friend Gienia, shared everything with me. I will always remember her generosity, even when she didn't have much to share.

In twenty-four hours I had gone from the Soviet gulag[4] to freedom to jail and to freedom again. And I wasn't yet nineteen years old.

I only stayed with the girls for a short time. When the weather turned warmer, I started getting itchy feet again – this restlessness has always been my problem. Another reason to leave was that I didn't want to burden the girls with my presence. They worked long hours, mostly in construction or as cleaning women – any work that didn't require any qualifications. I packed a few belongings that the girls had given me and set out to walk back to the city, where I found a job

---

4 Gulag is the Russian acronym for the Soviet system of forced labour camps. For more information, see the glossary.

in a small company that was making, or should I say, shaping, soup bowls and other things from clay. The pottery wheel was operated manually and I never really mastered it, although I tried.

By officially joining the labour force I was now entitled to half a kilo of bread a day. A Jewish girl from Romania on my crew, Esther, suggested that I share her allotted accommodations with her. I gladly accepted. When the first of the month rolled along, we were issued new ration cards. When Esther went to get her bread, I foolishly gave her my card without giving it a second thought. When she didn't show up for hours, I suspected that something had happened to her. I worried about her, but I should have been worrying about my own survival. At the end of the day, when Esther was still missing, as much as I hated to have anything to do with the police, I reported her disappearance. Upon hearing my story, they started to laugh. When I asked what the reason was for their enjoyment, they informed me that they already had my roommate in custody for theft and breaking and entering. All I wanted to know was what had happened to my ration card. The police told me that it had been sold on the black market. I was guilty – of being too trusting. Hadn't my life so far taught me anything? I guess not. My immediate problem was figuring out how I was going to survive for a whole month until a new card was issued. There was no such thing as a replacement.

I started thinking about the alternatives available to me. Maybe I should commit a minor crime and get myself jailed for a month until my new card was issued, thus ensuring that I wouldn't starve. I wasn't very familiar – although I should have been – with Soviet law, especially the punishment side of it. With my luck, I would probably be accused of something very serious, maybe even Article 58, for which my brother had paid with his life. There was a popular saying in the USSR at the time that people repeated only in private: "A person has to pray for life, but Comrade Stalin will provide years." Prison years, that is.

The Mines

With no ration card, I decided that my only real option was to volunteer to work in the mines. The work was hard and dangerous, but at least I would be entitled to one kilo of bread a day. This particular mine was extracting lead ore to be used in making war *materiél* that would be shipped by train to the front for the Red Army. In other words, my job was considered a part of the war effort and even though I had volunteered for the work, they considered me mobilized.

Before I started my first twelve-hour shift, I was given rubber boots, a rubber coat, a lamp and tools, but no helmet. The elevator took us down as far as it went and from there we had to descend by ladder on our own. This was very hard to do because we were loaded down with tools and the boots and coat we wore were very heavy. Everybody had rushed ahead of me when all of a sudden my oil lamp went out. I had no matches to rekindle it and just stood there for quite a while glued to the spot, afraid to move. I was terrified in the complete darkness around me and, at the same time, I was also afraid of being late for work. One experience of doing time in a hard-labour camp where you got punished even for being late for work, whatever the reason, had been enough for me. I don't know how long I stood enveloped in darkness until luckily another group of workers came along and relit my lamp. I learned not to go anywhere in the mine alone again, but always to travel with the group. I can't even begin to describe the terror and panic I experienced during that time. I was afraid that I might have to wait until the end of the shift twelve hours later. By that time I would probably have had a mental breakdown.

Our job was to load the wagons with ore left from the previous shift while drillers on our shift began their job. The blasting happened at midnight while we went to eat. On one occasion it was still early when we returned to start the second half of the shift and I was sitting on a pile of ore, waiting for the signal to begin loading the wagons. When our foreman showed up to check on everything, I saw him take out a pouch of *machorka* and a piece of newspaper and start rolling a cigarette. I also smoked then, but I never had my own cigarettes. Just as I got up and approached him for a smoke, the pile I was sitting on collapsed. A few seconds later and I would have been buried under tons of ore – I don't think they would have been able to dig me out alive. The foreman started yelling at his second-in-command for letting me sit in an area that wasn't secured. It's a miracle that I survived. Had I been a non-smoker, or if the foreman hadn't shown up at that exact time, I wouldn't be here to write about it. I might even go so far as to say that smoking saved my life.

This work was pure hell. We had to crawl on our bellies, chipping away at the ore. The ceiling was low with the water running down the walls, forcing us to work in knee-deep water. I was scared of how I was going to end up and it didn't take me long to realize that I might not survive under these circumstances. I was going to have to desert, which was a very dangerous thing to do, but I didn't think I had much choice. It was either keep working in the mine and possibly die, or escape. When my long month in the mine finally came to an end, I picked up my new ration card that entitled me to thirty kilograms of bread – treasure on the black market. I didn't show up for my next shift, but foolishly stayed overnight at my usual place. It was just a bit of space on the floor near a stove for warmth, but I was grateful for that.

I could have been easily picked up. Fortunately, the person in charge of finding absentees was a friend of mine, Tatiana, a Communist Party member. She had been only one year ahead of me at the *Tekhnikum*. She came to see me at dawn and told me to disappear immediately because the authorities were already looking for me. Tatiana had put herself in jeopardy for me. I still treasure a photograph she gave me with a dedication to me in Russian. She lived with her mother, who was always sitting with a Bible in her lap. When she found out that I was Jewish, she said that the world would come to an end when all the Jews went to live in a Jewish state.

I thought that was unbelievable, considering that the very existence of Jews was at stake. It was now the beginning of May 1944 and we had been hearing news of how the tide had turned in the war and things were looking positive for the Soviets. But we also began hearing some very depressing and alarming news about what had happened to Jews in the death camps and ghettos, and I started losing hope that I would ever find any survivors among my family when I returned to Poland. That was the feeling we all had and unfortunately it proved to be only too true. Yet here was Tatiana's mother with no doubt that the Jews were going to survive as a nation and have a state of their own.

Barefoot and with only the clothes on my back, I started out on a trek. I was equipped with a blackened pot in case I found something to eat and my treasured thirty-kilo bread card. The trouble was that I couldn't buy any food since I didn't have any money nor did I want to draw attention to myself. I just had to hang on.

My Luck Changes

Ust-Kamenogorsk

When I left Ridder for the last time, I followed the railroad tracks bound for Ust-Kamenogorsk, back to the area where the work camp was. The weather was pleasant and I was making good progress. Toward the evening I reached a *sovkhoz*, a state-owned agricultural settlement that is much larger than a *kolkhoz*, a collective farm. It looked quite prosperous and I was getting very hungry. I asked where and if I could get some food and shelter for the night and was sent to the manager's office. He was very suspicious of me, which wasn't surprising considering the way I looked. After all, spies come in all disguises and at that moment I was disguised as a hobo. The head of the collective interrogated me and I sensed trouble brewing.

His first question was why I was there and where I had come from. I did some quick thinking and told him that I had come from a different direction – not Ridder. I also said that I had been released from the camp in February and he asked how I had managed to live without any employment. My answer was that I had been surviving by panhandling. If I had told him that I was coming from Ridder, he might have figured out the truth and I would have faced either another term in the camp for absenteeism or – since I had been considered mobilized at the mine – an even more serious sentence for desertion. I must have sounded convincing because he believed me. Still, they put me in a locked cell with only rats for company throughout the night, gave me some food and that was that. I wasn't sure what the morning might bring and wondered if the manager had really believed me. At dawn, the door opened and a blond woman with a pockmarked face woke me up. She brought me some more food and told me to leave before her husband woke up. I didn't need to be told twice. I will always think of her as my guardian angel. It was another lucky escape.

I started walking, fortified with the food. Around what must have been noon, I met up with a woman and her two teenage daughters. For once I was glad to have some company, but that didn't last long when we saw horses coming toward us at a fast gallop. It turned out that these women had stolen some of the laundry from the *sovkhoz* where it had been left overnight to dry. They had the evidence with them and the three of them were taken back, probably to face a charge of stealing government property. Fortunately, they were decent enough not to involve me in this affair and, to my surprise I was allowed to continue on my way. Little did the authorities know that they had overlooked another, more serious offender – a deserter. Another lucky break for me.

By now it was late afternoon and I had to get some food. I saw an elderly woman cooking something outside her house and asked her if she would consider trading some food for my pot. She gave me some soup and a piece of bread, threw in a few raw potatoes and also let me spend the night on her porch. In those days, people were justifiably afraid of strangers – sometimes people were killed for food. Our ration cards may have entitled us to bread and other things like soup bones or cooking oil, but that was only on paper. I remember one time, as I was eating a piece of bread, I spied two young children watching me with hungry eyes, hoping that I would share some with them. But I couldn't share my first food in almost three days. This image will always haunt me. Now I had some potatoes, but having given away my pot, I couldn't cook them, so I ate them raw.

In the morning I started on the third leg of my trek without waking up my kind hostess. In the late afternoon I came to a huge river with a village on the other bank. The only way to cross it was to mingle with the workers from the village and get across on a barge. While waiting for them to finish their work, I ate some honeydew melons that I had stolen from a government field, as well as some green tomatoes. The tomatoes weren't ripe yet, but the melons were very sweet. I made it across the river without any questions being asked about my identity. People were used to seeing hobos.

When we got to the village, I came upon an older man sitting outside his home shelling green peas. He didn't refuse my offer of help and when he lit a *machorka papiros*, he gave me one. By that time I had become quite skilled at rolling cigarettes in newspaper. The man and his wife had a little plot of land, but they couldn't manage to work it themselves, so, because of their advanced age and the fact that their children were fighting the Nazis, the village had provided them with help. His wife was inside the house preparing supper for their mainly women helpers and invited me to share some of their food. I didn't need to be asked twice; tearfully and gratefully I accepted her kind offer. After we ate, it started to get dark as the sun disappeared behind the mountain and she invited me to spend the night. She was apparently not afraid to lodge a stranger. "We've lived long enough and worried enough about strangers in our lifetime. We don't scare as easily anymore," she told me. I probably looked more pitiful than dangerous. She put a mattress on the floor and gave me a down pillow and *perina*, a comforter. This unbelievable luxury kept me awake for a long time. It brought painfully back all the happy memories of my family life, never to be experienced again but never to be forgotten. I will always remember this wonderful old couple for caring enough for even a short while.

After breakfast – imagine! Two meals in so many days! – the couple arranged a ride for me to Ust-Kamenogorsk in a horse-drawn carriage driven by a farmer from their village. These last ten kilometres were the easiest of my 120-kilometre odyssey. The three-day trek had exposed me to many adventures and dangers, but nothing could have been worse than what I left behind.

When I reached Ust-Kamenogorsk I gave the man ten one-kilo coupons for bread as we had agreed. I sold another ten kilo-card on the black market and used the money to buy some food and milk. I sat on a bench to eat in the town's main bazaar, next to a man with a spinal deformity. It took me no time to recognize that we belonged to the same tribe and in the course of our conversation I asked him if he knew of any available jobs and places to live. He told me that the post office, where he was employed, was looking for a cleaning woman and that I should apply immediately. By then it was too late to go there right away, so I decided to wait until the next morning.

Another man who also looked Jewish to me struck up a conversation. I told him that I had just arrived in town and was looking for a place to stay for at least one night. He said that since he lived in a single room in the men's dormitory and worked the night shift, he would be happy to accommodate me for one night. I accepted gratefully and he took me to his room, warning me not to leave for any reason. I went straight to sleep but was startled awake from a deep sleep with the sensation that somebody else was in the room. Sure enough, the man who lived in the same room was standing over me, ready to get into the bed. I was really scared, but sat up and told him to go away or else I would scream. He didn't force himself on me and quietly left. I guess that I can't blame him for trying – in fact, under the circumstances, I think he behaved quite well.

My real problem arose when I needed to use the bathroom. I couldn't risk leaving the room and getting caught by the night guard, so I looked around for something to use as a chamber pot. I found a cooking pot, emptied my bladder and poured the contents out the window. I couldn't even rinse it out since there was no plumbing in the room. Somehow, I managed to sneak out early in the morning without anyone noticing me. Maybe I just looked like one of the boys who was going to work. I never saw the man again and avoided going to the marketplace in case he recognized me.

I went to the post office where I offered my services and was hired to start immediately. My friend the hunchback who had helped me get the job sat in his booth with a rifle checking people's identification. I often wondered whether the rifle was even loaded. My job was to wash the floors in the telephone and telegraph rooms and keep the office tidy. I also helped out in the office with filing and other clerical chores. The fact that I had been at a school for a year and a half helped me tremendously because I had picked up the Russian language very quickly. Before I knew it, though, the cold weather arrived and the unheated water I used for my job turned to ice. This was even more of a problem because I was also barefoot – I didn't have any shoes. My employers had graciously allowed me to sleep on a desk in the office, but the place was unheated at night. Things were really getting tough.

I remember the bookkeeper and his wife, both Armenians, quite fondly. She was very beautiful, with an amputated leg, and they were childless. They helped me a lot with the office work, but never asked me to come to their house. That may have been because my hygiene was non-existent. I still didn't have any place to take a bath. Again, fate intervened. One of the postal employees whose job was to collect letters from the seven mailboxes in town twice a day came down with a ruptured appendix and had to be hospitalized; I was offered her job temporarily. Not only was it quite easy, but as part of the job I was outfitted with a postal uniform – a sweater, quilted jacket, pair of pants and pair of warm *valenki*. I loved that job best of all because I wasn't stuck in one place and was more or less free between collections. I used my knowledge of Russian to the fullest, continuing to help out in the office in my free time. My employers offered to train me as a bookkeeper but I refused – I just couldn't see myself sitting behind a desk all day. I preferred the freedom that my job gave me. Strangely enough, years later in Canada, I ended up doing exactly the job I had turned down – sitting behind a desk doing bookkeeping – and loving it.

I had been doing the job for a while when I had another stroke of good luck. One of the girls on the mail delivery route had had to leave because her husband had been transferred to another city and the management at the post office offered me her job. It was an opportunity at precisely the right time – the girl for whom I had been substituting had recovered and was returning to work. Every piece fit.

I happily embraced my job. Once again I wasn't confined to a limited space. I was out all day by myself with no supervision. My delivery route was the largest in terms of the area it covered but it had the least amount of mail to deliver because it was mostly private addresses, not offices. I began work at eight in the morning, sorted my own mail and started my rounds by nine. If I hurried, I could be done by midday. I had to bring the bag with any undelivered mail back to the office and then I was free. I was well-liked and developed close relationships with the other girls. There weren't any men working in the sorting room. The few complaints I got were from customers who were annoyed when I refused to deliver letters or newspapers to a household with unchained dogs. To pacify the dogs, I sometimes had to part with some of my bread. The post office manager was an elderly lady who didn't always believe me, so one day she decided to come along with me on my route. When the dogs went after her, she agreed that my actions were justified.

During my free time I started speculating on the black market. The post office had its own store where we exchanged our coupons for bread rations. I bought the coupons on the black market, bought bread from the lady from the post office store, sold it on the black market and then the two of us divided the profit. We were both taking a terrible risk.

There was only one newspaper published in the city, the *Kazakhstanskaya Pravda*. It wasn't for sale because only members of the Communist Party could subscribe to it. I had a favourite customer who wanted to get the paper, however, so I found a way to take one each day from different customers who didn't have mailboxes. If anyone questioned me, I claimed that the wind had blown it away or that a dog wouldn't let me come near the box. The paper I took was destined for Mrs. Shkurenko, whom I came to call Aunt Katia. She was a Ukrainian who, along with her entire family, had been dispossessed of their farm during Stalin's collectivization campaign in the early 1930s. They had been singled out as *kulaks* and sent to Siberia. They were stripped of their Soviet citizenship and couldn't go anywhere. But after the outbreak of the German-Soviet war, their rights were restored and Katia's sons were taken into the Red Army to join in the fight against the Nazis.

Aunt Katia was a wonderful, warm person. I had lunch with her every day at noon and delivered her treasured contraband newspaper. You may call it stealing, but I called it survival. The paper was never thrown out, but was used for rolling cigarettes.

One day I went to Aunt Katia's house, not realizing that it was Easter. It didn't make any difference to me – I didn't know when it was Passover either. When I entered, she greeted me with, "Christos voskres!" (Christ has risen!) I didn't know what to say, but Katia told me that I was supposed to reply, "Na vieki viekov!" (Forever and ever!)

I reminded her that I was Jewish, but she already knew that. Still, she expected me to answer this way because, after all, Jesus was Jewish. I hadn't known that. I still can't make up my mind which of us was more ignorant. It must have been me. The question about the ancestry of Jesus never came up back home. His name was never mentioned. I had to come to the Soviet Union, a godless country, to find out anything about him.

Katia had killed a pig for the Easter holiday and made blood sausage. She offered to share it with me, but I refused and almost gagged just looking at it. It might have been my Jewish background. Not that

I ate kosher food in Siberia – where would I have gotten it, anyway? It was the blood I couldn't tolerate. Katia called me *maya malenkaya zhidovetchka*, my little Jewess. It sounded very endearing and we were fond of each other. She was very lonely too.

New Friends

Now that I was working steadily at the post office, my housing situation improved. Sometime in the fall of 1944 I moved into a house owned by an elderly man and his two daughters. Rima, the younger girl, was a tall, blue-eyed, blond, slim and beautiful. Lisa shared this bounty of good looks with her sister, although she was a little on the chubby side and more cuddly-looking. Their father occupied the small bedroom and the bigger one was shared by the three of us. Another room was rented to an actor, Frolov, who had come from Leningrad as an evacuee.

Frolov was everything I admired in a man. After all, I was now nineteen years old and not a kid anymore. He was very well-mannered and good-looking, although a bit on the stocky side. We spent hours talking about my favorite subject – Hollywood actors and actresses. He was very well informed. I loved to listen to him when he recited Russian poetry, which was mostly sad. I think that the Russian language is best suited for this art form. As an extra bonus I was able to attend for free every performance in which he was acting or directing.

Soon, another refugee enlarged our household. He was a colleague of Frolov's, also an actor from Leningrad, who was expecting his wife to join them soon. What a treat it was to watch them both onstage in their non-operatic version of *The Marriage of Figaro*.[1] Frolov starred as Figaro and his friend, whose name I don't recall, was Count

---

1   *The Marriage of Figaro* is a well-known comic opera composed by Wolgang Amadeus Mozart in 1786.

Almaviva. All the women were in love with them and I felt lucky to be close to them. The wife of Frolov's friend was expected to join the cast soon to play the part of Rosina, Count Almaviva's wife. I was eager to meet her. Nonetheless, something about the two friends' relationship began to make me feel uneasy. The door to their room was always closed when they were home and they were inseparable offstage. There were whispers that I didn't pay attention to – I wouldn't have understood them anyway.

Around this time my coworker Valentina Gornashkina, whom I called Valya, became my best friend. We were inseparable. She had a large family and I was always welcome in her home. She was intrigued by other people's culture and customs and absorbed everything like a sponge. I never saw Valya again after the war ended and I left the USSR, but I treasure her picture that she dedicated to me.

One evening I was out with Valya but decided to come home early because we had to be at our desks before eight o'clock in the morning to sort our own mail and start our deliveries. I let myself in quietly so that I wouldn't awaken the old man. The two girls were still out.

The door to the men's bedroom was slightly ajar, with a small bulb casting a weak light. I wanted to announce myself, but I stopped when I heard noises. At first, I heard the sound of a man engrossed in passionate rapture and sure enough it was Frolov. But then there was the sound of another voice, another deep and familiar voice. A morbid curiosity overcame me and I decided to take a peek undetected by the two lovers. It was definitely not Rosina in bed with Frolov. That night my idol fell off his pedestal and I lost my innocence. Things I hadn't understood before became clear to me. How naïve I was! I waited outside for the girls to come home and once they were inside I pretended that I had just arrived.

I still admired Frolov; his sexual orientation was of no concern to me. And it would have been silly for me to give up the free passes to the theatre. I acted as if nothing had changed and he never guessed that I had witnessed anything. Not too surprisingly, his comrade's wife never arrived.

Things were fine in the house until the girls' brother came home from army duty after suffering a slight injury that required him to walk with a cane. He had two distinctions – he liked to drink and he was a chess master for Eastern Kazakhstan. When he began to pay more attention to me than I desired, I decided that it was time to find other accommodations. The girls were upset, but I told them that I was leaving because the house had become too crowded, even though I really liked being with them.

I found a new place with a landlady – another Katya – who lived in a tiny house that was really only one room divided into a room and a tiny kitchen. I arrived at the house around the same time that Katya's niece joined the household to attend classes in a nursing school. As if the house wasn't crowded enough, a cow – also named Katya – lived in the tiny entranceway. Sometimes we also had weekend guests from the nearby *kolkhoz*. The man of the household was away fighting the Nazis along with other able-bodied men.

My postal uniform had a lightning bolt emblazoned on its sleeve to symbolize speed, although it took more than a month for a letter to get to us from the front. Sometimes when I delivered a letter the writer was already home recovering from injuries sustained at the front. Even worse, I occasionally had to deliver a letter from the army informing family members that their loved one had fallen defending the homeland. My mail route included twelve short blocks between two main arteries – Nabereznaya Street along the Irtysh River and Sadovaya Street. It was mostly residential and it so happened that many of the people along the route were involved in the arts. Some were musicians of the Philharmonic, some were actors from an excellent theatre and still others were managers of cinemas that showed mostly Soviet movies. I got to attend all these for free.

I loved going to the movies. There is one that I remember in particular – *Song of Russia* – an American film that came out in 1944 and featured the actor Robert Taylor. It was about a musician on tour who gets caught in Russia during the war and decides to stay to help boost the morale of the people. When I arrived in the USSR in 1940, any-thing that wasn't Soviet and especially anything Western was consid-ered suspect by the authorities. That attitude changed when both the USSR and the United States entered the war to fight their common enemy – Germany. With the Allies now fighting the Nazi scourge together, the official Soviet attitude toward the West lightened up and in the US, they started producing movies that were sympathetic to the Soviet Union.

Years later, the people involved in producing these movies had their lives shattered, courtesy of Joseph McCarthy, the US senator from Wisconsin.[2] As strange as it sounds, Taylor was one of the stars who testified at McCarthy's witch hunt, pointing a finger at his col-leagues and accusing them of belonging to the Communist Party. He surely helped to destroy these people's lives and careers; many never recovered emotionally or financially. Perhaps he had to justify his role in this movie.

One evening Valya and I had plans to go to a theatrical perfor-mance and I decided that I wanted to wear something more dressy than my uniform, so on pay day I went to the market and blew the whole lot on an American crepe dress and a new pair of shoes. Now that the Red Army was chasing the Germans back into their own lair, Soviet soldiers were taking whatever they could and sending the smaller items home. All of a sudden there was an abundance of cloth-ing on the market.

Unfortunately, it started pouring on my way to the theatre and as it got wetter and wetter my dress kept shrinking and creeping up. We didn't have polyester in those days. Soon the dress was well above my

---

2 In the 1950s, at the height of Cold War tensions between the US and the USSR, Republican Senator Joseph McCarthy accused many Hollywood writers, direc-tors, producers and actors of sympathizing with Communism and the Soviet Union. This led to the creation of a blacklist of people in the creative arts who found themselves barred from working in Hollywood.

knees and I kept pulling it down, to no avail. Embarrassed, I stopped paying attention to the performance and concentrated on trying to pull my dress down to its former length. Valya and I were the last to leave the theatre and Valya tried to help by walking behind me. I somehow managed to make it home in the rain, my skirt getting shorter and shorter along the way.

Once I was inside the house I saw that my calf-length dress was now above my knees. I must have invented the mini! I entered the hall very quietly since everyone including the cow was asleep. I got undressed, hung the dress on a line using a wire hanger, put the shoes on the little window ledge and retired to my little space to fall asleep. When I woke up, my first thought was to check if my dress had dried, but it wasn't there. It had disappeared, along with the wire hanger and my shoes. Did the cow chew up my dress? It was possible but not likely that she would also have chewed up a pair of shoes and a hanger. My new things were gone and I now had to wait a very long two weeks until I was paid again. Needless to say, I didn't eat too much during that time.

The War Ends

As 1944 came to an end and a new year began, the Allies were clearly winning the war. Since I was now nineteen, going on twenty, you would think that I would have developed an interest in the opposite sex, but that didn't happen. There just wasn't anyone I was attracted to – or maybe it was vice versa. All the young Jewish men I had known over the last five years lived in Ridder and most of them were married or had girlfriends. Some were on active duty or in the labour army.[3] I just couldn't find it in me to get involved with a non-Jewish

---

3 The term "labour army" (*trudarmiya* in Russian) was used in the USSR during World War II to refer to the compulsory labour service introduced in 1941. Conscription to labour duty was similar to military mobilization. For more information, see the glossary.

Russian man. Some of our girls did just that. They married, had children and stayed in Russia, feeling like outsiders. But this wasn't for me – I knew that I would go back to Poland. I can only imagine how they felt when they remained behind and the rest of us returned to Poland after the war. For them the link with our people was broken, never to be renewed.

I had no Jewish friends in Ust-Kamenogorsk, no one to speak Yiddish or Polish with – only Russian. I had mastered the language quite well and read Pushkin, Lermontov, Gorky, Shakespeare – in translation, of course – and other literary greats. The friends that I arrived in Ridder with were still there and I had kept in touch with them, but I stayed where I could make a living. I had become almost completely assimilated into Russian society, but I couldn't deny that the spark of *Yiddishkeit* was still there.[4] One cannot escape one's past.

On many evenings I walked through the quiet, deserted marketplace and listened to communiqués being broadcast from loudspeakers that named the cities that were being liberated in Poland. Among them was Lodz, my hometown, which was liberated on January 19, 1945. Unfortunately, I already knew that we had no reason to celebrate – by then the fate of our people had become known, although the full enormity of our losses would only hit us later. The frightening pictures began emerging as soon as the Red Army started liberating Poland. Other people suffered as well, but not in the same numbers as Jews. Still, murder is murder. There was plenty of evidence that Russian prisoners taken by the Nazis didn't stand a chance. They were executed upon capture.

Many prisoners who had somehow survived the Nazis died after being released, either from sickness or the change in their diet. They

---

4 *Yiddishkeit* means the "Jewishness" or "Jewish essence" of traditional Yiddish-speaking Jews of Eastern and Central Europe. It usually refers to the popular culture or practices of Yiddish-speaking Jews, and also to a feeling of emotional attachment or identification with the Jewish people.

had been starved for so long that their emaciated bodies couldn't tolerate the real food they were given by their liberators. The pictures shown in the newspapers or in the newsreels were horrific and utterly shocking. How could such cruelty and inhumane treatment of other human beings be perpetrated by a so-called nation? Of course, they had many collaborators all over Europe – Quisling in Norway, the Vichy government of occupied France and others.[5] The list goes on and on.

In the early morning of May 9, 1945, we woke up to the sound of singing, music and a lot of noise. The war was over. We were free! I joined the crowd gathering in the city square to celebrate. I knew that I had nothing to be elated about, but I was happy that the killings had finally come to an end. Although many people would be able to pick up where they left off years ago, that was unfortunately not true for us Jews. I had no idea when I would be able to return to Poland or what awaited me there. Like others, I began writing letters to the Red Cross in Geneva, but mine had yet to be answered.[6]

Even in the face of horrors, life goes on. And yet, like millions of others, my own wounds have never healed. I can close a door to my room and to my present, but not to my past, especially now as I try to retrace my life as far back as I can. I shed bitter tears, silently I cry. My mourning is endless. What life could have been, if only … but life belongs to the living until it runs its course.

------

5 Vidkun Quisling was a Norwegian politician and officer who actively collaborated with the Nazis and was appointed by them to lead Norway from February 1942 until the end of World War II. The Vichy government was the government of France from July 1940 to August 1944 that cooperated extensively with German occupiers, most notably in the deportation of French Jews.

6 The International Committee of the Red Cross, based in Genevea, acted as one of the main agencies in Europe during and after the war for locating and getting information about missing people, and in particular about Jews and concentration camp detainees.

Malaria

With the war over, my landlady's other niece arrived to join our growing household. It was time for me to leave, especially since Katya anticipated another arrival, namely her husband, who would soon be discharged from the army. I started looking for yet another place to live – the last one, I hoped, before returning to Poland. Luckily, Mrs. Shkurenko, the exiled Ukrainian *kulak* I called Aunt Katia, took me in. She lived at Ulica Kuznechnaya No. 38. She was a caring and lovely person and I was accepted by her daughters like a family member. Both of her married daughters' husbands were still serving in the Red Army, as were her own two sons, and only her single daughter lived with her.

When I moved in with Aunt Katia, the long Siberian winter was finally over. It was the spring of 1945 – spring comes in late May and June in Siberia – and the snow was melting and creating swamps that were a boon for malaria-causing mosquitos. Even if you were only bitten once, you were in danger of contracting the disease. Being young, I thought that nothing could touch me. I soon found out how wrong I was in assuming that I was immune – I became infected.

One morning I woke up earlier than usual, feverish and shaking like a leaf. As sick as I felt, I knew that I still had to report for work at the post office. I didn't want to face another prison term of six months or more – I had to show up to let them see I wasn't faking my illness. Somehow, I made it, but the desk was piled with mail that had to be sorted. I was getting sicker by the minute and found it impossible to go on.

Seeing how sick I was – I was running a fever of nearly 42 degrees Celsius – my supervisor sent me home, assisted by one of my co-workers. My only stop was to get my daily ration of bread at the store. If I didn't redeem my coupon the same day, it would expire; the coupons had dates on them. When we reached the marketplace my co-worker met a friend and deserted me. I just sat down on a step clutching the bread and people kept coming up to me to ask if I was selling it. With my very high fever, I dozed on and off constantly until almost sundown. Then the fever started to drop and I became more lucid, although I was still feeling extremely weak. When I tried to stand up, I experienced a feeling of blindness from the fever. When I described it to a doctor later, he told me that this wasn't unusual with a drastic fluctuation in body temperature.

I don't know how long I sat on the step, unable to move. Surprisingly, nobody stole my bread, which they easily could have done – I wouldn't have been able to resist. A policeman approached me and accused me of being a speculator, which, as I have said, was a very serious offence in Soviet Russia. I found it impossible to convince him that I was holding my own ration; I even showed him my card, but to no avail.

"I see you very often at the market, selling bread," he said.

"That might be true," I replied, "but not today." He wasn't convinced and took me into custody. I couldn't believe it – I had never been caught in the act of actually selling black market bread and now I was being arrested when I was innocent. I followed him slowly, still very weak from the fever. He left me in the care of a family that operated a kiosk that was one of the few private enterprises allowed by the regime. They sold honey, milk and other non-rationed food items for which coupons weren't required.

"Watch her while I round up a few more criminals. I'll be back," he told the shopkeeper.

We waited until it was almost dark, but there was still no sign of the lawman. One of the family members locked up the kiosk and when they saw how weak I was they decided to take me home with them. The entire family had been evacuated from Ukraine and their house was filled with musical instruments. They saw my interest and asked me if I would like to hear some music. I have always loved music and was delighted by their offer. The only instrument I had ever learned to play was the little bit of guitar I had picked up in Ridder.

The mother of the family sat down at the piano and her husband picked up a violin. The son played accordion, but I don't remember what instrument the daughter played. As soon as I heard the first few bars of the melody I immediately recognized the song "Hatikvah" (The Hope), that would one day become the anthem of the State of Israel.[7] We Jews didn't have a state and the way things were going, I didn't dare to hope that we ever would or that the Jewish people would survive. The news that kept reaching us was terrible.

When the family finished playing, none of us made any comment about the musical selection. We didn't mention who or what we were – we just understood each other and tacitly acknowledged our common connection, our belonging and our yearning. Now I understood why the policeman had left me with this particular family and didn't come back to get me. He also recognized our connection and perhaps had some sympathy for us. I shared a small meal with the family and left. I never did re-connect with them again.

The following day, I went back to work as usual delivering mail, but the day after that, the shakes hit me again. I was taken to see a doctor and was diagnosed with tropical malaria. The symptoms occur every second day and last from sunrise until sunset. How long it would go on was anybody's guess.

The treatment for malaria was quinine, but my prescription couldn't be filled because there was none available. Fortunately, the area I serviced on my postal route included a drug store, the only one in the city, and the manager was able to provide me with a quantity of the drug. The only problem was that she could only give it to me in bulk, as a loose powder. I figured that if a little bit helped, then twice the amount would help me twice as much. I put my self-made dos-

---

7 "Hatikvah" was composed as a poem in 1878 and later set to music and widely adopted by Zionist groups in Europe as an anthem of the Zionist movement. Like Ann and this family, most Jews in Eastern Europe would have been familiar with the words and the melody.

ages into pieces of newspaper, which made them easier to swallow and also avoided the very bitter taste. How wrong I was to do this! The overdose of quinine that I took turned my skin and the whites of my eyes yellow and affected my hearing for awhile. The doctor warned me against continuing the medication lest I do serious damage to my liver.

The bouts of malaria went on all through the summer, which is very short in Siberia and could also often be very hot and humid. Winter could set in quite early – it sometimes started snowing in August. The ground never really had a chance to dry out completely, creating swamps and wet patches everywhere. It was the only time during my six years in Siberia that I actually welcomed the onset of winter. I hoped that it would bring me relief from malaria because the mosquitoes would disappear. I couldn't worry about what next spring was going to bring.

Finally, one morning I woke up shaking only slightly and hoped that, maybe, I was better for the time being. I was right. This was the only bout of malaria that I had, and while it lasted, it was awful.

My Last Year in the USSR

Career Change

The Germans didn't only kill people but also destroyed much of what was in their path and took anything they could eat or wear just for the fun of it. The economies of the Soviet Union's western republics – such as the Ukraine and Belorussia, among others – had been completely devastated during the occupation. Crops were burned, livestock were slaughtered, homes were destroyed. The government in Moscow now issued orders that every *kolkhoz* in other regions had to contribute cattle to those republics to help revitalize their economies. Kazakhstan also received these orders.

In the summer of 1945 volunteers signed up to accompany the livestock westward and soon the cattle trains were ready to move. By the time I heard about it, a few of the transports were already en route. I decided to take a leave of absence from my postal job and try to get on one of the transports. In some ways I was ready for a new adventure, but I also thought this might be a way to get home. Before leaving the post office, though, I secured a promise from them that if things didn't work out, they'd take me back. I registered for the transport, was accepted and began my new career as a *pastuch*, a shepherd. We were stationed outside the city of Ust-Kamenogorsk where tents had been set up along the Irtysh River and waited for the cattle to arrive. The weather was good, sunny and warm. The earth had dried out, minimizing the threat of mosquitos and another bout of malaria. Because we were so close to the river, bathing wasn't a problem.

The first shipment of cattle arrived and the animals were immediately branded by putting buttons in their ears with a stapler. I noticed that cows are very territorial creatures – they always occupied the same spot at night and if a newcomer tried to take it, the interloper was kicked away. Our group consisted of people from many different backgrounds and one woman in particular stands out in my memory. She was a refugee from a big city, a prim and proper widow with a seven-year-old son. I found it strange that they had hired her and let her bring her child along. I'm sure that she had never been close to a cow before, but just like the rest of us, she was very anxious to go home by any means possible. I remember that she once recounted the advice she had been given about how to get the cows to obey her command. She had been told to shout "Fuck off!" to urge them on. She innocently followed the advice and said that it actually did help – she actually did manage to get some cooperation from the cattle.

Every morning more cattle arrived. Our task was simple – early in the morning we took the herd to the pasture where the grass was high and moist. Around noon we took them to the river to drink and cool off. Then back to the pasture, and by late afternoon, we drove them back to settle for the night.

Our diet was very bland. Instead of bread we were issued flour for the whole week. Of course, we had plenty of milk. We heated it and added the flour which created a kind of mush that the Romanians call *mamaliga*. It wasn't much to my liking. I managed to exchange my rations of milk, cheese and butter for fish and eggs with the local people. I also managed to drink a lot of fresh milk straight from the cows, not worrying that it wasn't pasteurized or that it may have come from a diseased cow. Sometimes we even had meat when the veterinarian, a non-volunteer, occasionally slaughtered a newborn calf. He would sign a document stating that the animal had died of natural causes.

All around us were fields of tomatoes that were still green. I couldn't eat them, but the others weren't so particular and helped themselves – or to put it plainly, they stole them. We greedily eyed the fields of ripe honeydew melons and once, close to midnight, we raided the fields and stuffed ourselves with the delicious fruit. We ate it all right then and there because we didn't want to leave any evidence at the camp. The supervisor of the collective settlement showed up the next morning and accused us of taking the fruit, but finding no proof, he left, not very convinced that we were innocent. We didn't do it again.

After we brought the herd home in the late afternoon, we were given milking pails and stools. On my first day, one of the girls who must have been from a farm showed me how to milk the cows. It looked quite easy, so I sat down, put the pail under the udders and started pulling. Nothing came out. The teats were very slippery, but I didn't give up. The little bit that I did manage to get out landed either on my face or in my lap. By that time, even the cow got impatient with me. She kept turning her head toward me contemptuously and finally kicked me to the ground, overturning the empty pail and swishing me in the face with her tail. I wasn't sure if she was punishing me for my incompetence or if she was simply chasing away the flies. When one of the girls came back to collect the pails and discovered that they were still empty, I was assigned to keeping the tents clean instead. I guess I wasn't cut out to be a milkmaid.

One day, when the weather had turned very hot, we were about to take the herd to the river to drink and cool off when suddenly one cow's tail went up and she started a stampede. The rest of the herd scattered in all directions. When calm was finally restored, we looked at each other, stunned. What do we do now? We thought. We had lost government property – around fifty head of cattle, including some bulls. Having no choice, we returned to the camp empty-handed. We were told in no uncertain terms to find the herd and bring it back.

It was still light so, armed with a rope, I set out in search of the escapees. Almost immediately I came upon a cow without horns that looked like one of ours. But when I approached it, I realized that this cow wasn't one that we had branded. But what the heck, I thought. A cow is a cow. I put the rope around her neck and started pulling, but she was stubborn and wouldn't budge. By the time I was able to persuade her to follow me back to camp, I had almost strangled the poor beast.

When I got back to camp, the leader made no comment. The next day, however, the cow's owner showed up to reclaim his property, threatening to involve the police and charge us with theft. We just told him that he should be grateful that we had milked his cow otherwise the milk would have spoiled. Realizing that there was some truth to it, he left with his cow and even thanked us. Later that day, the herd returned on its own. How, I'll never know.

A few weeks later we were told that no more cattle were going to be shipped since the quota had been reached. By this point, I couldn't say that I was disappointed – for one thing it was getting too cold to sleep in the tents. At the end of August in Siberia the weather can change from pleasant and warm to snow in a matter of minutes. The work was good while it lasted – I had gotten plenty of fresh air and healthy food to eat – but I was ready to return to civilization. I asked the authorities on the cattle detail for permission to leave and was very happy to hear that it was granted.

Before we disbanded, we were given one more task. We had to watch a herd of sheep overnight and then milk them in the morning. I stayed away from this chore – I hated to go near these stupid beasts. Whenever they heard dogs barking at night, they all started running in one direction and our job was to bring them back. I definitely wasn't cut out for farm work. I couldn't understand why humans were needed for this exhausting, unpleasant chore when sheepdogs would have done nicely.

Back to the Post Office

I prepared to return to my old job at the post office, which I now appreciated even more after my summer experience. Still I have to admit that even though I found the way of life very primitive, I was glad to have experienced it. My landlady, Aunt Katia, gladly took me back. I now called her *Mamushka*, "Mommy."

In all the time that I lived with Aunt Katia she never charged me rent. Instead, she asked me to help provide her with wood for heating, which I did. Although we were surrounded by rivers, mountains and endless forests, it was hard to get wood to burn for heating, and getting food remained problematic though things were improving. Our ration cards supposedly allowed us to get meat and butter, but this was only true on paper. All we were actually able to get was bones and some oil. And not everybody could even get these things, although having friends in the post office's store meant that I could. Still, white bread now started to appear again, something we hadn't seen in years.

One of my continuing problems was that I still wasn't able to get rid of the lice that had been plaguing me for years and I never had any extra underwear. Aunt Katia was aware of this and she pressed whatever meagre clothes I possessed with a hot iron to kill the nits, the lice eggs. Thus, I was finally able to say goodbye to the problem that I had lived with for so long.

I have often wondered why it was that I was so accepted by many non-Jews when certain Jews had actually caused me to suffer. Still, I craved the closeness of real community and many times felt like a prodigal daughter, always trying to return home no matter how many times I ran away, always drawn back to our common past.

The long, snowy, cold winter now set in, but regardless of the weather, the mail had to be delivered and life went on as usual. When the temperature dipped very low, there was practically no wind and I was in constant danger of getting frostbite. I kept my head covered completely with a scarf with only one eye showing, but still my breath kept icing up my eyelashes and brows. I had to keep scraping my eyes to enable me to see where I was going in snow that was well above my knees. By the time I got home, my *valenki* were soaking wet. To dry them for the next day, I would put them in the oven, but the embers would burn holes in them. Stuffing newspapers in them didn't help either.

There was so much snow on the ground that what was a second floor in the summer became a basement in the winter and the drifts almost buried the electric poles. Things weren't much better when spring came because of the mud. Rain made the soil very sticky and slippery and we could hardly lift our feet out of the mire. My shoes kept sticking in the mud and coming off. Most of the time I walked barefoot, carrying my shoes for two reasons – so that I wouldn't fall and to save my shoes. The streets weren't paved and there were only a few wooden planks along the main streets to serve as sidewalks.

I made it through another winter. Fortunately I liked my job. I ended up working at the post office longer than anywhere else be-cause it was challenging and there was never a dull moment. Maybe I was also finally growing up. I was never hungry anymore. People along my route filled up my mail bag with all kinds of food. I contin-ued to make myself useful at the post office. Every now and then, they received a shipment of vodka in barrels that must have previously contained kerosene because the vodka reeked of it. I'm sure that the kegs hadn't even been rinsed. In order to get the vodka out of the bar-rels a thin tube was inserted and someone had to suck on it to get the flow going. I was sometimes the person asked to do this and got more than I bargained for, namely, a mouth of kerosene-flavor vodka. Even the fumes sickened me, but I overcame it.

The importance of my position as a letter carrier also gave me some additional responsibilities. Many times I noticed two letters with the same handwriting addressed to two different women – one the sender's wife and the other probably a girlfriend. No matter how hard the wives tried to bribe me to divulge names, I never did. When we took this job, we were all sworn to secrecy and I never betrayed the trust. I had had enough troubles to last me a lifetime and was afraid of the consequences if I ever strayed from the rules again.

As I mentioned, it took about a month for a letter to arrive from the front and sometimes men were discharged before their last letter reached the family. That was cause for a celebration and a homecoming party. I was often asked to join the party and, of course, I couldn't refuse, could I? Only once did I get drunk and fall asleep with the bag of undelivered mail beside me. When I woke up the next morning, I ran out to deliver the rest of the mail. When I showed up before eight o'clock, however, my supervisor, an elderly lady, was waiting for me. It was a very serious offence to keep the mail bag overnight, but since it had never happened before and she liked me, she let me off with a warning. Fortunately, no one else was in the office yet, so we kept it to ourselves and nobody ever found out what I did. I probably wouldn't have been so lucky the next time.

That winter turned out to be my last one in the Soviet Union. I had lost six and a half years of my life. By now I was fairly certain that my family hadn't survived. None of the many letters I wrote to the Red Cross in Geneva were ever acknowledged or answered. Either they were overwhelmed by the number of enquiries or they were indifferent. It no longer mattered because we knew what had happened.

Because of my years of malnourishment I didn't menstruate for three years, which was a blessing in disguise since there were no sanitary napkins to be found. I later found out that this phenomenon had happened to a lot of girls. Now, however, I decided to do something about it and booked an appointment with a female gynecologist. One day before I was set to see her, though, I didn't have to worry about it anymore – my period returned. It seems it was a case of mind over matter. The body is an amazing thing.

I did have other medical problems that didn't clear up as easily. I came down with an infected lymph node on the side of my neck.

It became full of pus, but since I had no fever I couldn't get a release from work. I was in constant pain and the strap of my mail bag kept rubbing against my neck. I was sent to a clinic to get an ultraviolet lamp treatment, but one day, while I was getting undressed, I squeezed the lump and it burst. The doctor wanted to surgically drain it, but I didn't allow it. The sore kept closing up, but I kept squeezing it until it cleared up. The episode left me with limited flexibility and I remain unable to bend my head to the left.

Although I continued to do my usual chores I was getting impatient. I longed to return home and rumours had begun to circulate in early 1946 that we would be able to go back to Poland soon, probably after the winter. When it was finally announced that we could register for the trip home, I encountered a frustrating delay because I didn't have any papers identifying me as a Polish citizen. My documents had all been taken away by the NKVD when my brother was arrested back in June 1940 and were never returned. I had no proof of who I was. When at first I wasn't able to register, my friends in Ridder started to hear rumors that I had a Russian boyfriend and had decided to stay. Of course, the thought never entered my mind – I didn't have a Russian boyfriend or anyone else in my life. As soon as the second registration opened up, I rushed to put my name on the list. Again, I was sent to a doctor to determine my age and again he concurred with what had been previously established: that I was two years older than I actually was, a fact that they decided just by looking at my teeth. Only after I returned to Lodz and got my birth certificate did my real age became a matter of record once again.

While I waited to be allowed to return to Poland, I decided that I needed to make some money. I was very interested in buying some of the mostly German clothing that the returning soldiers were bringing back as spoils of war. A man I knew was selling tobacco on the black market and wanted to expand his operation, so I opened a branch for him. Once I was outfitted with a bag filled with tobacco and a measuring glass, I was open for business. My first customer was a mobilized soldier on crutches who took some of the stuff, rolled it in a newspaper, lit it and took a few puffs. He decided that he liked it, asked me to put a cup of the tobacco in his pocket and started walking away without paying: When I ran after him to demand payment, he obliged me by hitting me in the face. He said that while he had been fighting for us, we had all been at home getting rich. Then and there I folded my business, losing the ten rubles that I had to repay my boss, and returned everything to the dealer.

I was determined not to give up so easily the second time I tried my hand at business, however. The manager of the drugstore in town gave me a few bottles of pure *spirtus*, alcohol, to sell at the market. Unknowingly, I had again put myself in danger. The drugstore manager hadn't dared to go to the market herself because what she had given me was stolen merchandise. Pure alcohol was a rare commodity and was still being rationed, so I hoped to sell it quickly and come back for more. It was Sunday and the kiosks were closed. There were just a few of us *spekulanty*. A young man approached me and asked the price. I told him and he tried to bargain me down. When I refused, he asked me to follow him behind the kiosk. I sensed trouble. He showed me his police identification and told me that he wanted to celebrate his friend's return and wouldn't report me if I gave him a good price. By then, I would gladly have given him the alcohol for free, but he was decent enough to pay for his purchase. Maybe he wasn't a policeman at all. Again, I returned the rest of my supply to the druggist. This was my last attempt at business in the USSR. I retired permanently.

Meanwhile, the people at the post office tried everything to keep me there. They promised to send me back to school and even went so far as to offer me a kiosk selling cosmetics and the popular malt beverage *kvas*. But I was anxious to go home and start looking for the remnants of my family. I still hoped that by some miracle I would find someone even though the war had been over for a year and I hadn't heard one word from anyone.

Finally, one day in May 1946, I was informed that my papers had arrived and were waiting for me at the police station, which was right across the road from the post office. I was very excited. Not able to wait another minute, I ran across the road to the police station to pick up my travel papers as soon as I heard. When I got back fifteen minutes later, the post office's big boss was waiting for me. I had committed another crime. *Progul* was still being enforced. I had been absent from my desk during working hours and for that I was docked 25 per cent of my wages for a period of three months. I was lucky though – no prison term this time.

Leaving Kazakhstan

I left the Soviet Union soon after I got my papers. I am probably still on the Soviets' Most Wanted list for escaping without paying the penalty that I had incurred for my brief absenteeism. I kid you not – the gnawing fear of being arrested stayed with me until we crossed into Poland. I was constantly afraid that the authorities would take me off the train and charge me again with escaping custody. I even worried that they might detain me in Poland because it was now occupied and controlled by the USSR, and on its way to becoming a Communist country.

My luggage consisted of a bag of *suchary*, which is dried bread rusks, a jar of melted butter, very little clothing, a pair of size twelve boots and nothing else. I took very little away with me but I left behind what should have been the best years of my life and a young brother buried in an unmarked grave, dead of tuberculosis at the age of twenty-three. I hadn't accumulated much in my six and a half years in the Soviet Union. I was traumatized and scarred, but I left Russia with my life. Under the circumstances, I couldn't ask for more.

Our day of departure was a beautiful May morning. I had already said fond goodbyes to my coworkers at the post office, to my neighbours and to the people on my mail route. I was sorry to leave my landlady and her family. We hugged and kissed, promising to write, which I did, at least for a while. I also wrote to my friend Valya from the post office for a time, but I had to stop soon after the war because the Soviets once again became suspicious of anything and anyone foreign and I didn't want to get any of my friends into trouble for receiving letters from abroad, even from a friendly country like Poland.

Mamushka stood on the balcony, waving and throwing kisses. I kept turning around and she was still there. When finally I came to the bend of the road, I turned around one more time, but couldn't see her anymore. At that moment, my ties with the Soviet Union came to an end.

I was the only person from Ust-Kamenogorsk registered to go with this transport and the rest of our group wouldn't be arriving from Ridder until the next day. There was only one train a day going west and for the time being I was alone at the railroad station. It was going to be a long wait, so I made myself comfortable on a bench. I soaked my little package of dry bread in *kipiatol*, hot water, which was provided in every station for tea.

In the middle of the night, a man in a uniform appeared in front of me and asked to see my documents. I complied and he took a look at the papers that had my picture on the Russian part; the other half was in Polish. He ordered me to come to his office, but I refused, sensing something fishy. I demanded that he tell me what was wrong with my papers and he walked away when he couldn't come up with an explanation. Where did I get the nerve to act as I did? I don't know. He could have forced me to go with him – the station was almost deserted. I fell asleep, only to be woken up by a loud cry. A young peasant girl had been approached by the same man and, terrified, she went with him to his office, where he raped her. I never found out what happened afterward because the train with our people from Ridder arrived, some of whom I hadn't seen in years. So much had changed, so much lost.

When we had started our journey in the winter of 1940, the

month-long trip east across this vast land was very difficult and cold. It was now May 1946. The return trip west also took a month, but with a big difference. The air was pleasant and warm, and the doors of the cattle cars were open on both sides. Most of the time, I sat on the edge of the doors with my feet dangling over the rails and observed nature, now in full bloom. We sang Russian, Polish and Jewish songs, trying not to think of the horrors awaiting us upon our return to Poland.

The cars were outfitted with bunks and I don't remember if we had mattresses or blankets, but it didn't matter – it was summer. There were no toilet facilities and it was still easier for the men; the women still suffered. Sometimes when the rail was cleared of traffic, the train went a whole day without stopping. When it finally came to a stop, we all dashed outside, men next to women, it didn't matter. What a scramble! We never looked at each others' faces – all you could see was a row of exposed bums. It was humiliating, but what choice was there? We couldn't afford to be modest.

Many times, when we expected the stop to last longer, we got out our dry rations, built a fire and prepared to cook. But if the train suddenly and unexpectedly started to move, we had to leave everything – the pots, pans and half-cooked meals – and jump aboard. A few times we got to go to a *banya*, a bathhouse. We were given a small piece of soap, which was a precious commodity, and sometimes we were even given a cooked meal.

There were mostly families in my car and they didn't favour me with much attention. I was viewed as an outsider, having lived apart from them all these years. Each car had a person assigned as a leader and ours was Pan (Mr.) Korzuch. He wasn't very sensitive and didn't like me at all. When the car leaders were giving out basic necessities such as sanitary napkins to the girls, I didn't get any.

One evening I went to join some other young people in another car for some fun. We sang and made plans for the future. Some of them were engaged to be married. I didn't realize how late it was when I returned to my car until I found it locked. My fellow travellers wouldn't let me in so I had to look for accommodation in another car. When I returned to my car in the morning, all I got were dirty looks. I wonder what they were thinking of me. Were they wondering about my virginity? I wasn't going to tell them that I was as pure as the snow in Siberia. I wouldn't give them the satisfaction. Then again, they probably wouldn't have believed me. But I really didn't care – I was now a grownup, responsible for my life and my behaviour.

We were slowly making our way west. We stopped for a day just past Barnaul in Novosibirsk and noticed that the buses there didn't have any glass panels; instead they were covered with plywood. We passed other cities, but didn't stop. We reached the Ural Mountains, which mark the border between Asia and Europe, and continued our trip west. In Moscow we stopped long enough to sightsee. Some people lined up at Red Square to see Lenin's embalmed body in the mausoleum, but I wasn't interested.[1] Instead, my group went to see Moscow's beautiful Metro. We also visited the war museum, walked along the banks of the Moskva River, and were free to walk around the city on our own.

We didn't see any evidence of the devastation caused by the war until we reached Minsk, the capital city of the Belorussian Republic, which had been completely destroyed along with its Jewish population and the lives of countless others.

But we hadn't come face-to-face with the reality yet. That would hit us soon.

Almost a month after we left Kazakhstan, we finally reached Brest-Litovsk, formerly in Polish territory and now on the Soviet side of the new border between Poland and the Soviet Union.[2] The Soviet

---

1 Red Square is the famous central city square in Moscow located next to the Kremlin, the official residence and offices of the USSR's, and now Russia's leaders.

2 As part of the post-war territorial settlement agreed by the Allies in 1945, Poland's eastern border was moved westward and 180,000 square kilometres of territory was ceded to the Soviet Union.

border guards came aboard the train, checked our papers, clipped off the Russian part with our pictures, and went through our belongings. Naively and stupidly, I had agreed to help one man take some American twenty-dollar gold coins across the order by hiding them on my person. Luckily, the guards didn't go through my belongings. I guess I didn't look too prosperous. Had they found the coins, I would have been in a lot of trouble for being an accessory to smuggling. The possession of any gold currency was illegal. I would have been sent back and probably wouldn't have been allowed to return to Poland. Just to show how naïve I was, this man whom I had helped was one of the people who wouldn't let me back into our car when I arrived back late. He never rewarded me, even though I could have easily kept the coins. Who would he complain to? Hadn't life taught me anything?

One of the young border guards asked me why I was going back to Poland and I told him that I was going to look for my family. He said that it was useless because all the *Yevrei*, Jews, had been killed. He was angry that I had decided to leave the Soviet Union because, in his eyes, this was the best country in the world. His final words to me were, "*Nitchevo*, never mind, when we fight the Americans, you will come running back to us and we will give you shelter again." For many years, when the Iron Curtain was up, I was afraid that his prediction might come true.

Poland

Welcome Home?

We were finally back in Poland, but it didn't feel like home anymore. A Polish woman came to the train and took us to a nearby field where, she told us, all the Jews from this particular village had been shot and buried. We walked on the shallow grave and found many bones. One of the men from our transport said Kaddish, the mourner's prayer. Unfortunately, it would become a very familiar chant. What we saw here reinforced our fear as to the fate of our families. We returned to the train with very heavy hearts. We still didn't know where we would eventually wind up, but it didn't seem to matter any more.

While we were still near the border one of our men, who had a hunched back, went to the well to get some water for his twin sons. He was attacked and beaten up by a violent gang who stole his gold ring. We stood and watched in terror. One night soon afterward the train didn't stop at all until morning and when it did, we saw, to our horror, that the cars containing Jews had been marked with a *Magen David*, a Star of David.

This was a shattering experience for me. In all honesty, I had never been discriminated against as a Jew in the Soviet Union. It was true that I was hungry, homeless, dirty and friendless, but none of that was because of who or what I was. We had all shared a common misery in the Soviet Union, but never for a moment had it occurred to me to bite the hand that fed and protected me. It was true that I had lost a brother, but this was due in large measure to one of our own coreligionists.

I had to overcome my disappointment at the greeting we received. The brutal attack at the border made me doubt that I had made the right decision in returning to Poland, my homeland. My ancestors had lived there for centuries and had been welcomed by a Polish king, but unfortunately, even with the war over, it hadn't taken long for hate to rear its ugly head.[1] We were never referred to as Jewish Poles – only as Polish Jews, a distinction that Hitler also had no trouble making.

Our train continued on. We were warned that we would be travelling through dangerous territory where there were lots of soldiers of the illegal AK – the Armia Krajowa or Home Army – hiding in the woods and attacking trains.[2] They were underground fighters who had fought the Germans as partisans during the Nazi occupation of Poland, but now they were fighting against the Soviet-imposed Communist regime that presently controlled the country. As we plodded along westward, we came to towns and villages that had been part of Germany before the war but now belonged to Poland.[3] We were headed for the port city of Szczecin (Stettin in German). In

---

1 During the Crusades in the thirteenth century, Poland served as a haven for European Jewry because of its relative tolerance. In 1264, Prince Boleslaw issued the "Statute of Kalisz" that guaranteed protection of the Jews. King Kasimierz ratified the charter and extended it in the fourteenth century when freedom of worship and assembly was granted to the Jews.

2 Formed in February 1942, the Armia Krajowa was the largest Polish resistance movement in German-occupied Poland in World War II. For more information, see the glossary.

3 In mid-1945, the Allies agreed to a post-war territorial settlement in Europe that compensated Poland for the loss of her eastern territories to the USSR with German territory from the provinces of Silesia, the southern part of East Prussia and Pomerania (where Stettin/Szczecin is located).

the area there was absolute calm – not a sign of life. During one stop, some of the people from our train ran down into a valley hoping to take some spoils of war from the village, whatever might have been left by the former German occupants who had either been forced out or fled on their own, afraid of repercussions from the advancing Red Army. The passengers came back mostly empty-handed – all they brought back were some mattresses. Anything of value had been looted a long time ago. After all, it was now June 1946, and the war had been over for a year.

Taking the mattresses proved to be unnecessary. When we reached our final destination of Szczecin, we were assigned rooms in furnished apartments that had belonged to Germans who had fled back to the Fatherland. The Germans were terrified, knowing that the day of judgment was upon them. I shared an apartment with a young couple who had a very small child. They were very anxious to have another baby and there were nights when I couldn't sleep because of the noise. They didn't much care who was around. I slept at the foot of their bed, but they were absolutely unhindered by my presence. Except for the lack of sleep, none of this really bothered me. My thoughts were elsewhere – I was waiting for an opportunity to go to Lodz on my quest to find survivors from my family. A lot of my friends went on to Germany, but this wasn't my goal.

Szczecin was very clean and had been relatively untouched by the war. The water pipes of the building we stayed in hadn't yet been connected to the main line, however, so there was no running water. Everyone had to line up at the well in the courtyard to get water. There were still some Germans in the city and when they saw me – a Jewish girl! – approach with my pail, they parted, letting me go ahead. I felt like Moses parting the Red Sea. Nonetheless, a few weeks among the defeated German population – they were repatriated later – was enough for me. I saw a murderer in every one. I remember hearing the saying, "A German is either at your throat or at your knees" and wondered to myself, how long will their humility last? Only time would tell.

I was determined to get to Lodz. I had been going to the Jewish centre at Szczecin every day to check the names of survivors, but I hadn't found any from my family. Part of the problem may have been that I was so young when the war began that I didn't remember the names of many of our more distant relatives. But I had to face the fact that my name didn't appear on any lists either. Nobody was looking for me.

When I decided that it was time to go back to Lodz, I went to the Jewish centre to pick up a few articles of clothing – including a pair of purple high-heeled shoes with ankle straps – my first pair! I could hardly walk in them. In Russia I had mostly gone barefoot in the summer and worn felt boots in the winter. I was now beginning to feel like an independent young lady, although not enough to make up for all those lost years. The Jewish centre had a very large warehouse of donated goods that had been provided by the United Nations Relief and Rehabilitation Administration as well as by American Jews. They also gave me enough money for my train fare and a little bit extra.

I went to say goodbye to my friends, most of whom were now going on to the Displaced Persons camps in Germany.[4] From there they would emigrate to whichever country would admit them. Many of those who were now married would give birth to their children in their new countries.

Lodz Memories Redux

The overnight train I boarded to travel to Lodz was so packed that at first I had no place to sit. I found a little spot next to a Polish soldier and we talked most of the night. The coach was dark and he prob-

---

4 Displaced Persons camps were facilities established in Germany, France, Italy and Belgium – some located in former concentration camps – where stateless Jews and others were housed. Some refugees remained in these camps for several years while they waited for permission to emigrate. For more information, see the glossary.

ably didn't realize that I was Jewish. Or maybe he did. He asked for my address in the city, but as soon as we arrived, I slipped away from him and disappeared into the crowd. I got off at the Koluszki train station in Lodz, the same one where Shoel and I had boarded the train to Warsaw on our way to safety in November 1939. I walked along familiar streets that had been untouched by war. During the Nazi occupation Lodz had been incorporated into the Third Reich and renamed Litzmannstadt after the German general Karl Litzmann who had captured the city during World War I. Accordingly, Lodz had escaped the fate of Warsaw, which was flattened by the Nazis.

I walked toward the Jewish shelter on St. Jacob's Street, which was in the part of the city that had been the Jewish area before the war. Most of us pathetic remnants were being housed and fed there until we were able to get established. This building was undamaged but, unlike the rest of the city, everything else in the surrounding neighbourhood was in ruins, including the old, beautiful synagogue that I used to walk by every morning on my way to school. On my way to the shelter, I was followed by two young Poles who kept trying to trip me by stepping on my heels and calling after me, "Sara!"[5] I wasn't afraid of them, just disgusted by their behaviour and the mentality of the people amongst whom we had lived for many centuries. Once again, I began to wonder if I had made the right decision in coming back to Poland. The only thing that brought me here was the hope that maybe there was a slight chance that some members of my family had survived. For months I kept checking, but I had no luck.

When I reached the shelter amongst the ruins, I was assigned a bed and given a light meal of soup, bread and tea. Now that I was settled, I was ready to explore the parts of the city that had escaped

---

5 It was common for Nazi authorities to call all Jewish women "Sara" and Jewish men "Israel," a practice that began with the August 1938 decree that Jewish men and women bearing first names of "non-Jewish" origin had to add "Israel" and "Sara," respectively, to their given names on all official identity documents.

destruction. I started with the Plac Wolności, Freedom Square. The statue of Tadeusz Kosciuszko that had stood at its centre was long gone, dynamited by the Germans in 1939 when they first took the city. I walked the four streets that branched out from the square, starting with Nowomiejsa, New City Street. Before the war, I had sometimes delivered finished blazers that my father had tailored to a retailer there.

I passed by the house where my beautiful, curly-haired friend Tymianko had lived. We had once been in the same class and had many of our lessons together. Still further was the photography studio where I had had my picture taken with my mother for a passport when we went to Berlin to visit Aunt Sarah and Uncle Yumi. I walked past the storefront where my father had bought me my first raincoat. How I remember impatiently waiting for rain!

The billboard with a poster of the Dionne quintuplets advertising Palmolive products was still up; Polish women were selling flowers and others offered scales for people who wanted to weigh themselves. The famous clock above the city hall was still working; before the war a lot of young people had waited there for their dates to show up. Yard goods stores still sold beautiful fabrics. Cafés served tempting fancy pastries; stores were stocked with kielbasa and other delicacies; ice cream parlours were full of treats. I couldn't afford any of them; I could only look. Nothing seemed to have changed for the general population. For the Jews, everything had changed.

It was time for me to go back to the shelter and have my bowl of soup, bread and tea. As incredible as it sounds, I experienced real hunger in Lodz. The Centralny Komitet Zydow w Polsce, the Central Jewish Committee of Poland, sent me to work in a knitting factory and when noon arrived on my first day, I was ready to faint, not having eaten anything but a slice of bread and tea since morning. I had no money to buy food. I couldn't face the looks of pity from my co-workers even though they offered to share their food with me. I still had some pride left. I didn't show up for work the next day. What could they possibly do to me? There was no *progul* in Poland.

I was able to find only two of my former classmates when I got back to the city. One had tuberculosis and moved to Israel. The other, Bronia, left Poland in the 1960s and went to Montreal, where she lived with her family. But I never found a single family member.

Soon after I arrived, I felt compelled to visit all the places where we had lived before the war. During the first fourteen years of my life I had lived in four different places. The fifth move was to my sister's place when the Germans occupied our city. First I went to our building on Polnocna, and to my shock, I saw that the side of the street where we lived, the side with the odd numbers, had been completely sheared off as if somebody had taken a knife and cut it very neatly. The rest of the tenement was untouched. Strangely, the Lodz ghetto had started on the other side of the street, the side with the even numbers.

Next, I went to our tenement with the courtyard at Podrzeczna No. 12, the site of so many of my childhood memories. I reached what I assumed was the building but there was nothing to remind me of my previous life. It was just a pile of rubble, with not a soul in sight. Unrecognizable. I kicked the dust and it filled my nostrils. The sky was cloudless, the sun hot on this summer afternoon. I would have preferred clouds, rain and my own tears. Everything was dry. A well-known Yiddish song that I remembered from my childhood kept haunting me and I began humming it:

Where is the little street,
Where is the room,
Where is the little girl that I love?
There is no more little street,
There is no more room,
There is no more little girl that I love.[6]

---

6 Ann Szedlecki's translation of the Yiddish song "Vi iz dos geseleh" by Sholom Secunda and Israel Rosenberg (1926).

Suddenly I went back in time as other forgotten things from my childhood began flooding in. I started remembering things connected with our street very vividly.

I don't remember how long I sat there remembering and seeing images from my past life. I could have gone on forever. I kept expecting some kind of noise, but the dead are silent. Suddenly, I heard voices echoing in this complete devastation. I opened my eyes, my face wet. With a heavy heart I came back to reality. I said goodbye to the ghosts of my past, although the mourning will never stop. I never returned to the ruins of the ghetto again, although I lived in Lodz for the next four years.

The time had come to rejoin the living.

A Chance Encounter with Pani Borzykowski, Headmistress of Public School No. 132 for Jewish Girls

The tragic events of the war showed that we were all equal.

Sometime after I had returned to Lodz, I took a walk along the main streets and stopped in front of Narutowicza Street No. 20, at the Europa Cinema next to the Tabarin nightclub with its revolving dance floor. The front of the building had an entrance to the concert hall where the Lodz Philharmonic Orchestra was performing that day. I bought a ticket and took my seat behind a couple. The woman wore a hat with a huge feather, which was very fashionable at the time, and it obstructed my view. I was just about to lean over and tap her on the shoulder to ask her to please remove her hat when she turned sideways and my jaw dropped – it was Pani Borzykowski, my former school principal.

In spite of living through three months of Nazi terror, six years under Stalin's murderous regime (including six months of indescribable misery at a hard-labour camp), I was still afraid to intrude on Mrs. Borzykowski's inner sanctum. Was there still a child in me? I sat behind her in awe, afraid to tap her on the shoulder, or engage her in conversation, afraid to be reprimanded. Time stood still. I felt fourteen again, standing as if nailed to the floor, holding the school's banner and afraid to interrupt her.

It never occurred to me to ask, "How did you survive?" It wasn't necessary. We were proof enough that we had. I survived in the Soviet Union and I heard that she had been hidden by her husband, a Polish Catholic. We never exchanged a single word. I never met her again.

Epilogue

If my brother, Shoel, had succeeded in crossing the border into the Soviet Union the first time he tried, I wouldn't be here to tell this story. I would have fallen victim to the Nazis along with the rest of my family.

Timing is certainly everything. We Jews adhere to a proscribed period of one month of heavy mourning for family members. I was never able to observe this religious custom for my brother because of my situation. Yet I later realized that exactly one month after Shoel's death, on the day that I would have gotten up from this period of mourning, the Warsaw Ghetto Uprising took place. On April 19, 1943, Jews rose up and fought back and died fighting, but not before taking out five thousand shocked and terrified Nazi soldiers.[1] Were any of my family still alive in Warsaw then? Did this uprising wipe out the rest of my family? I will never know.

Chance and choice matter too. My group was part of a tiny number of Jews who volunteered to work in Siberia, rather than being part of a roundup or deportation. We were part of an even smaller minority who didn't head back home once we realized the hardships of Siberia. Was it luck? Or was it what we Jews call a *nes*, a miracle?

---

1 Resistance to the Nazis began in the Warsaw ghetto on January 18, 1943, and continued until May 1943. On April 19, 1943, about 750 organized ghetto fighters launched an armed insurrection. The largest single act of violent resistance by Jews during the Holocaust, it was crushed on May 16, 1943.

There are many things that have mystified me about my own story, some that I have been able to find an explanation for and others not. One such incident involved the Nazi officer who tore my twenty-zloty bill in half at the border when we were crossing into Soviet territory on our way to Bialystok. I learned years later that the zloty had been withdrawn from circulation by the Nazis in December 1939, which coincided with the time of our departure from our parents, and hadn't been replaced with any other form of currency. I don't know what we would have done had we known that our money was worthless and that the Nazis had stolen all our family's assets. We might have turned around and gone back home.

How my family ended up in the Warsaw ghetto instead of the one in Lodz remains a complete mystery to me. I learned that they had ended up there from a brief mention in one of my sister's heavily censored letters, and I also know that they first went to Bolimów and then to Lowicz, but I don't know the circumstances of these moves or how long they stayed. The last address I have for them was in the Warsaw ghetto at Nowolipie Street No. 22. This was the information I received in their last letter to me, the one I received on the very day that Germany attacked the Soviet Union – June 22, 1941. Their street is mentioned in *The Warsaw Diary of Chaim Kaplan.*[2] This beautiful, handwritten Hebrew-language diary was found in the ruins of the Warsaw ghetto and is one of the few written eye-witness accounts of life in the ghetto that survived the war. Kaplan mentions a raid carried out by the Nazis on July 31, 1942, that targeted all the buildings on Nowolipie Street and ended with the deportation of all the residents. I can well imagine – no, I cannot, I cannot imagine the terror they must have felt, hearing the murderers, heavy boots coming closer and closer. Did the Germans take my parents, sister and niece then, or

---

2   Chaim A. Kaplan, *Scroll of Agony: The Warsaw Diary of Chaim A. Kaplan* (New York: McMillan 1965). Kaplan's entry about the raid on Nowolipe Street is found on page 335.

did my family get a reprieve until the next misery-filled day? Were they even still there? Did my little niece cry out in hunger or was she too weak to do even this? Were they able to give her some food, part of their own meagre ration, perhaps? Who was the first to go, or did they stay together until the end, giving each other solace? These questions and all the rest of them will remain unanswered forever.

I know from my family's letters that Aunt Sarah's husband had a mental breakdown and was admitted to a psychiatric hospital near Lodz. But I learned later, to my horror, that these people and those in other institutions were not treated but rather were among the first to be murdered by the Nazis as a mass human euthanasia experiment.[3]

When World War II broke out I was fourteen years old. From that time on I have considered myself to be a war orphan. When I returned to Poland in 1946 I was twenty-one years old, alone and still an orphan at heart. So many unfulfilled dreams, ambitions, hopes of happiness.

In my teen years in the Soviet Union I never really had a close friend, but there were many people who showed me kindness when it mattered most. Still, the process of growing up and surviving had been a very serious business and a very lonely one. I realize now how much I missed important things like having a boyfriend, going steady or even just dating. Maybe stealing a few kisses with someone interested in me or the other way around. Unfortunately, this wasn't to be either. When I first read *The Diary of Anne Frank*, I compared our lives. She was born on June 12; my birthday is June 13. We were only two years apart. Our initials were the same – A. F. We both kept

---

3 The Nazis began a program to kill institutionalized people with physical, mental or emotional handicaps in 1939. The program was implemented mainly in the Third Reich, which included Lodz after November 1939, as opposed to German-occupied areas where murder was generally executed by much more brutal methods. The program to murder institutionalized patients was implemented near Lodz at the Kochanowka psychiatric hospital from March to August 1940.

diaries. Hers survived; she didn't. I survived, but my diary was probably burned in Lodz during the liquidation of the ghetto. My diary contained a lot of silly entries, one of which I particularly remember: "Nothing exciting is happening in my life."

My growing up years should have been the best years of my life. Instead, they were devoted almost entirely to finding a piece of bread, a warm meal or a place on the floor near a *piechka*, a stove, to put my head down during the cruel Siberian winters, or to fighting off malaria-causing mosquitos in the hot summer. Nevertheless, during my more than six years in the Soviet Union I lived among people with whom I had no trouble communicating in spite of differences in language, background and religion. I consider myself very lucky that I didn't live – or I should say die – according to Germany's plan to murder all Jews. The rest of my family and millions of other Jews weren't so lucky. In my case the Nazis didn't succeed in adding another name – mine – to their list of names or more ashes to those that accumulated in the death camps.

My mother performed the highest maternal sacrifice and act of deep love by letting me go to the Soviet Union with my brother, thus saving me from falling into the clutches of the murderous Nazis. Was it maternal premonition?

Dearest Mother, Wherever You Are,

Not a day goes by that I don't think of you. I shed tears when I look at your dear face, looking at me from the only picture I have. Time will never erase your cherished features from my memory. For saving me I am forever grateful. Shoel wasn't so lucky.

Mother, to you I can bare my soul as never before. There was a time when I was so hungry, homeless, lonely and desperate that I was fully prepared to do the unthinkable – for me, at least – namely to sell myself for a meal. It wasn't difficult to find an accommodating prospect, even with the way I looked. But when it came time to actually do it, I couldn't. Needless to say, I was just as hungry as before, but my virginity and pride were intact.

I had promised my mother, of blessed memory, the very last time that I saw her, that I would be decent. It was very hard to keep that promise, but I am glad that I made sacrifices that helped me maintain my self-respect. I am proud that I kept the promise I gave to my mother and I know that I made her proud.

These were very trying times. I fought for survival and won in spite of incredible difficulties. I overcame them and, I hope, I became a better person because of them. Yet I still stagger under the weight of my pain and loss. Why was I favoured? My whole family was killed by the Nazis and my only relative, my brother, lost his life while I was safely tucked away in Siberia, far from the raging war and the devastation suffered by the Jews and others.

Although in the Soviet Union we were never strangers to hardships, my existence as a Jew was never threatened. Everyone had the same fortune and fate of hunger, sometimes homelessness, and loneliness. If only, if only…. If only more had followed in our footsteps into the USSR…. If only the US had entered the war sooner…. How many lives – and not just Jewish lives – might have been saved?

The picture that was enclosed with the last letter from my family is my most treasured possession. It shows my parents, Liba and Shimshon Frajlich, my two aunts, Sarah and Tauba, my sister Malka and her two-year-old baby, Miriam. The dress that my sister is wearing in the picture was well known to me. I helped her pick out the fabric and the style because she trusted my taste. My little niece's dress was remade from an old red woolen dress of mine. My mother is wearing her plain burgundy dress and my father has his good, double-breasted suit on. It is very hard to look at this picture and not remember bits and pieces of our wonderful, and sometimes not so wonderful, times together. It is hard not cry. These are the most important faces and names in the album of my life – shattered and gone without a trace except in my memories, and in these stories.

Glossary

afikoman (Hebrew; from the Greek word *epikomian*; literally· afterdinner festivities) The *afikoman* is a half-piece of matzah that is broken in the early stages of the Passover seder and set aside to be eaten after the meal. It is usually hidden by the seder leader or one of the other adults and children are encouraged to try to find it as part of a game to keep them interested through what is often a long ritual meal. The *afikoman* is the last thing eaten at the seder. *See also* Passover; seder.

Anders, General Wladyslaw (1892–1970). Wladyslaw Anders was a general in the Polish army before and during World War II and a member of the Polish government-in-exile in London after the war. A cavalry commander on the eve of World War II, Anders was taken prisoner by Soviet forces when they invaded Poland in September 1939. When Germany attacked the Soviet Union in June 1941, Anders was released by the Soviets and asked to form an armed force of Poles living in the USSR to fight alongside the Red Army. By 1942, this force, known as the Anders Army, included approximately 72,000 combatants – among whom were at least 4,000 to 5,000 Jews. Political tensions between Soviet authorities and the Polish government-in-exile, as well as shortages of weapons, food and clothing, led Anders to convince Stalin to let him take his forces to the Midddle East in August 1942. From

1943 to 1946, Anders' men provided the bulk of the Second Corps of the Polish Armed Forces that fought under British command in Italy.

Armia Krajowa (Polish) Also known as AK or the Home Army. Formed in February 1942, the Armia Krajowa was the largest Polish resistance movement in German-occupied Poland in World War II. Although the organization has been criticized for anti-semitism and some factions were even guilty of killing Jews, it is also true that the AK established a Section for Jewish Affairs in February 1942 that collected information about what was happening to Jews in Poland, centralized contacts between Polish and Jewish resistance organizations and supported the Relief Council for Jews in Poland. Members of the AK also participated in the Warsaw Ghetto Uprising in 1943, both outside the ghetto walls and by taking a direct part in fights inside the ghetto with Jewish fighters, and led the failed Warsaw Uprising of August 1944. Between 1942 and 1945, hundreds of Jews joined the AK.

Article 58 The notorious 1928 statute in the Soviet Union's Penal Code that introduced the formal notion of the "enemy of workers" and was used by the Soviet secret police to arrest those suspected of "counter-revolutionary activities." The Article became the justification for the imprisonment and death of a huge number of innocent people. Sentences under the Article could last as long as 25 years and were often extended indefinitely without trial or consultation.

bar mitzvah, bat mitzvah (Hebrew; literally: one to whom commandments apply) According to Jewish tradition, boys become religiously and morally responsible for their actions and are considered adults for the purpose of synagogue ritual at the age of thirteen. A bar mitzvah is also the synagogue ceremony and family celebration that mark the attainment of this status, during which the boy is called upon to read the Torah publicly. Practiced for centuries for boys, in the latter half of the twentieth century liberal Jews also began to hold similar ceremonies and celebrations for girls – called a bat mitzvah – which takes place at the age of twelve.

bolnitza (Russian) A medical clinic.

Bund (Yiddish, short for Algemeyner Yidisher Arbeter Bund in Lite, Polyn, un Rusland, meaning the Jewish Workers' Alliance in Lithuania, Poland and Russia). Jewish social-democratic revolutionary movement founded in Vilna in 1897 to fight for the rights of the Yiddish-speaking Jewish worker in Eastern Europe, advocate Jewish cultural autonomy in the diaspora and champion Yiddish language and secular culture. In interwar Poland, the Bund served as one of many Jewish political organizations that also had affiliated schools, youth groups and sports clubs.

Central Jewish Committee in Poland (in Polish: Centralny Komitet Zydow Polsce, or CKZP) The organization that existed between 1944 and 1950 to represent Jews in Poland to state authorities. It was also the coordinating body for aid and social services to Holocaust survivors in Poland.

challah (Hebrew) Braided egg bread traditionally eaten on Shabbat and other Jewish holidays.

cholent (Yiddish) A traditional Jewish slow-cooked pot stew usually eaten as the main course at the festive Shabbat lunch on Saturdays after the synagogue service and on other Jewish holidays. For Jews of eastern-European descent, the basic ingredients of *cholent* are meat, potatoes, beans and barley.

chametz (Hebrew; in Yiddish, *chometz*). The bread, grains and leavened products that are not consumed, sold or owned on the Jewish holiday of Passover; a product that is made from wheat, barley, spelt, rye or oats and that has undergone fermentation as the result of contact with liquid. *See also* Passover.

chuppah (Hebrew) The canopy used in traditional Jewish weddings, usually made of a cloth (sometimes a prayer shawl) stretched or supported over four poles. A chuppah is meant to symbolize the home the couple will build together.

cohen ([Hebrew, pl. *cohanim*] In biblical times, *cohen* was the word for priest. The cohanim were responsible for worship ceremonies in the days of the Temple in Jerusalem. In the post-biblical era, a *cohen* refers to people who trace their ancestry to the family of Judaism's first priest, Aaron, the brother of Moses. They occupy a special ritual status in Judaism (such as reciting certain blessings in synagogues). According to Jewish traditions, particular rules apply to a *cohen* such as having no contact with dead bodies and not marrying a divorcee or a convert to Judaism.

collectivization The policy pursued after 1929 in the USSR to reorganize agriculture by instituting state ownership of land or creating collective farms. Collectivization was achieved by forcible means and with much loss of life among the peasantry (including the death of several million peasants from the artificial famine created by the policy). Resistance to collectivization was very strong, especially among the prosperous peasants, or *kulaks*. In response, Stalin ordered that food rations be cut off to peasants in areas of opposition, especially in the Ukraine. Hundreds of thousands of those who opposed collectivization were executed or sent to forced-labour camps. Many peasant families were also forcibly resettled into exile settlements in remote areas. Collectivization did not live up to Stalin's expectations and the agricultural sector in the USSR suffered from low productivity throughout the Soviet period.

communal oven Cooperatively shared oven, common in prewar Jewish communities in Europe, that was used for Shabbat cooking. Larger than the ovens people would have at home, the oven could accommodate the challahs – special braided egg bread tradition-

ally served on Shabbat – and the other delicacies that were reserved for Shabbat and special holidays. The communal oven also
allowed people to have a hot meal on Saturday afternoons without
requiring observant Jews to light a fire, which is proscribed on the
Sabbath. Instead, the oven would be lit on Friday before sundown
and kept on a low heat for the entire Sabbath.

Dayenu (Hebrew; literally: it would have been enough for us) A traditional song of gratitude that is sung during the ritual meal, or
seder, held at the beginning of the Jewish holiday of Passover. The
song is over one thousand years old and lists the many gifts given
by God to the Jewish people. *See also* Passover; seder.

Displaced Persons Camps Facilities set up by the Allies at the end of
World War II to provide shelter for the millions of people – both
Jews and non-Jews – who had been displaced from their home
countries as a result of the war.

Dzigan and Szumacher Well-know Yiddish language comedians in
pre-war Poland who survived the war in the Soviet Union and
returned to Poland after it. In 1948 they performed *Unzere Kinder*
(Our Children) with child survivors of the Holocaust then living
in an orphanage near Lodz; the performance was subsequently
made into Poland's last Yiddish feature film. In the early 1950s,
the comedic pair moved to Israel, where they remained until their
deaths in 1980 and 1961 respectively.

feldsher (Russian) Medic or physician's assistant. Healthcare professional who provided many medical services in the Soviet Union,
mainly in rural areas.

fifth column A term first used by the Nationalists in the Spanish
Civil War of 1936–1939 to refer to their supporters within the territories controlled by the Republican side. Because these people
were helping the four columns of the Nationalists' army, they were
deemed to be their "fifth column." Since that time the expression

has been used to designate a group of people who are clandestinely collaborating with an invading enemy.

Four Questions Four questions that are recited at the start of the Passover seder, usually by the youngest child at the table. As much of the seder is designed to fulfill biblical obligation to tell the exodus story to children, the ritual asking of the questions is one of the most important at the seder. The questions revolve around the theme of how this night of commemoration of the exodus is different from other nights – e.g., Why do we eat unleavened bread? Why do we eat bitter herbs? The readings from the Haggadah that follow answer the questions and in doing so tell the exodus story. *See also* Passover

Free City of Danzig (German; Free City of Gdańsk in Polish) City state and seaport situated at the mouth of the Vistula River on the Baltic Sea, located about 340 kilometres from Lodz and 500 kilometres from Berlin. Danzig belonged to Germany prior to World War I but was made an autonomous "Free City" by the peace settlement following it. Under the authority of the League of Nations throughout the interwar period, Danzig/Gdańsk was a major point of contention between Germany and Poland, with the latter maintaining special economic rights in the area and acting as the representative of the city state abroad. In September 1939, the Germans occupied and immediately annexed the city. The city endured heavy Allied and Soviet air bombardment during the war and was largely destroyed during the Soviet capture of the city in March 1945. In the post-war settlement agreed by the Allies, the city became part of Poland.

fufaika (Russian) Quilted jacket.

ghetto A confined residential area for Jews. The term originated in Venice, Italy in 1516 with a law requiring all Jews to live on a segregated, gated island known as Ghetto Nuovo. Throughout the Middle Ages in Europe, Jews were often forcibly confined to gated Jewish neighbourhoods. During the Holocaust, the Nazis forced Jews to live in crowded and unsanitary conditions in run-down districts of cities and towns. Most ghettoes in Poland were enclosed by brick walls or wooden fences with barbed wire. The Warsaw ghetto was the largest in Poland with over 400,000 Jews crowded into an area of 1.3 square miles; the Lodz ghetto was the second-largest, with 160,000 inhabitants. Ann Szedlecki's family were incarcerated in the Warsaw ghetto.

Great Synagogue of Lodz (also known as the Deutsche, German or Reform Shul) Built in 1887 by a group of city's leading industrial-ists and wealthy merchants, the Great Synagogue was one of the most visible of the Jewish institutions in Lodz. Known for its architecture and beautiful interior furnishings and mosaics, it was one of the largest structures in the centre of the city. The congregation of the Great Synagogue included Lodz's leading industrialists, wealthy merchants, bankers, professionals and members of the Jewish intelligentsia who drew inspiration from the ideas of the German Jewish enlightenment that flourished in the mid-nineteenth century. Along with three other well-known synagogues in Lodz, the Great Synagogue was completely destroyed by the occupying Nazis in November 1939.

gulag (Russian; acronym for Glavnoe Upravlenie ispravitel'no-trudovykh Lagerei, meaning Main Administration of Corrective Labour Camps). The term refers both to the bureaucracy that operated the Soviet system of forced labour camps in the Stalin era and to the camps themselves. The Soviet system of forced labour penal camps greatly grew in size during Stalin's campaign to turn the Soviet Union into a modern industrial power and to collectivize agriculture in the early 1930s; millions of prisoners were incarcerated. Gulag camps existed throughout the Soviet Union, but the largest camps lay in the most extreme geographical and climatic regions of the country (such as in the Arctic north, the Siberian east and the Central Asian south). Prisoners endured hard labour, violence, extreme climate, meagre food rations and unsanitary conditions, all of which resulted in high death rates. Historians estimate that from 1934 to 1953 over a million prisoners died in Gulag camps.

Haggadah (Hebrew, pl. Hagaddot; literally: telling) A book of readings followed at the Passover seder service. *See also* Passover.

Hatikvah (Hebrew; literally: the hope) A poem composed Naphtali Herz Imber in 1878 that was set to a folk melody and adopted by early Zionist groups in Europe, including the First Zionist Congress in 1897, as their anthem. When the State of Israel was established in 1948, it was unofficially proclaimed the national anthem, but became so officially only in 2004.

Kaddish (Aramaic; literally: holy) Also known as the Mourners' Prayer, Kaddish is said as part of mourning rituals in Jewish prayer services as well as at funerals and memorials.

kolhoz (Russian) Short for *kollektivnoe khozyaistvo*, meaning collective farm. *See also* collectivization; *sovkhoz*.

kosher (Hebrew; literally: proper) Fit to eat according to Jewish dietary laws. Observant Jews follow a system of rules known as *Kashruth* that regulates what can be eaten, how food is prepared and how meat and poultry are slaughtered. Food is *kosher* when it is deemed fit for consumption according to this system of rules. There are several foods that are forbidden, most notably pork products and shell fish.

Kosciuszko, Tadeusz (1746–1817) Polish military leader who fought in the American Revolutionary War as a colonel in the Continental Army, and also led a failed 1794 uprising against Imperial Russia that came to be known as the Kościuszko Uprising; regarded as a national hero in Poland, Lithuania, Belarus and the United States.

Komsomol (Russian; short form of Kommunisticheskiy Soyuz Molodiozhi, meaning Communist Union of Youth) The youth movement of the Soviet Communist Party established in 1918. Geared to youths between the ages of fourteen and twenty-eight, the Komsomol functioned as a means of transmitting Party values to future members. Members of Komsomol were frequently favoured over non-members for scholarships and employment, and becoming a young officer in Komsomol was often seen as a good way to rise in the ranks of the Party.

Kristallnacht (German; literally: night of broken glass) A series of pogroms that took place in Germany on November 9–10, 1938. Over the course of twenty-four hours, ninety-one Jews were murdered, 25,000–30,000 were arrested and deported to concentration camps, two hundred synagogues were destroyed and thousands of Jewish businesses and homes were ransacked. Planned as a coordinated Nazi attack on the Jews of Germany, Kristallnacht is often seen as an important turning point in Hitler's policies of systematically persecuting Jews.

kulak (Russian) Term coined in the USSR during Stalin's campaign of forced collectivization to refer to a prosperous or land-owning peasant. *See also* collectivization.

kvas (Russian) Mildly alcoholic beverage made from rye bread popular in the USSR – and in Russia and all the former Soviet republics to this day – as well as in other Eastern and Central European countries.

labour army (in Russian, *trudarmiya*) Compulsory labour introduced in the USSR in 1941. Conscription to labour duty was similar to military mobilization. The conscripts worked in dangerous, heavy industries such as coal mining, petroleum extraction, railroad construction and ammunition, and were frequently housed in the same conditions as those in prison camps. One notable group of workers in the labour army were ethnic Germans from the Volga region who were drafted en masse in 1942; about one third of them did not survive the war.

machorka (Russian) Homegrown tobacco.

Mariacki Hejnał Traditional five-note Polish tune also know as the Krakowian Hymn. According to a popular twentieth-century legend, a guard on the higher of the two towers on the Mariacki church in Krakow sounded the alarm that the city was about to be attacked during the Mongol invasion of 1241 by playing the Hejnał. The city gates were closed before the city was taken but the bugler was shot in the throat and could not complete the tune. This is why it now ends abruptly. The Mariacki Hejnał was traditionally played from the tower twice a day at dawn and dusk, although it is now played on the hour. Since 1927, there has been a live broadcast on Polish national radio of the hymn every day just before the news at noon. This is what young Ann heard on her Aunt Tauba's radio when she was convalescing from the mumps.

matzah (Hebrew, also matza, matzoh, matsah; in Yiddish, matze) Crisp, flatbread made of white plain flour and water that is not allowed to rise before or during baking. Matzah is eaten as a substitute for bread during the Jewish holiday of Passover, when eating bread and leavened products is forbidden. *See also chametz*; Passover.

May Day Also known as International Workers' Day, May Day is celebrated on May 1 in many countries around the world in recognition of the achievements of workers and the international labour movement. It was first celebrated in Russia on May 1, 1917. In countries other than Canada and the US – where Labour Day is considered the official holiday for workers – May Day is marked by huge street rallies led by workers, trade unions, anarchists and various communist and socialist parties.

mikvah (Hebrew; literally: a pool or gathering of water) A ritual purification bath taken by Jews on occasions that denote change, such as before the Sabbath (signifying the shift from a regular weekday to a holy day of rest), as well as those that denote a change in personal status, such as before a person's wedding or, for a married woman, after menstruation. The word mikvah refers to both the pool of water and the building that houses the ritual bath.

Molotov-Ribbentrop Pact. *See* Treaty of Non-aggression between Germany and the USSR.

nachalnik (Russian) Director, boss, chief.

nes (Hebrew) Miracle.

NKVD (Russian; acronym of the Narodnyi Komissariat Vnutrennikh Del, meaning People's Commissariat for Internal Affairs). The NKVD functioned as the Soviet Union's security agency, secret police and intelligence agency from 1934 to 1954. It was renamed the KGB (the acronym of the Komitet Gosudarstvennoy Bezopasnosti, meaning Committee for State Security) in 1954 and served the same function until 1991. The organization operated with a military hierarchy in its stated dual purpose of simultaneously defending the USSR from external dangers from foreign powers and the Communist Party from perceived dangers within. Under Stalin, the pursuit of imagined conspiracies against the state became a central focus and the NKVD played a critical role in suppressing political dissent.

Nuremberg Laws. Laws passed in 1935 in Nazi Germany to strip Jews of their civil rights as German citizens and separate them from Germans legally, socially and politically. Under "The Law for the Protection of German Blood and Honor," Jews were defined as a separate race rather than a religious group. Whether a person was racially Jewish was determined by ancestry (how many Jewish grandparents a person had). Among other things, the law forbade marriages or sexual relations between Jews and Germans.

Passover (in Hebrew, Pesach) One of the major festivals of the Jewish calendar, Passover commemorates the freedom and exodus of the Israelite slaves from Egypt during the reign of the Pharaoh Ramses II. Occurring in the spring, the festival lasts for eight days and begins with a lavish ritual meal called a seder during which the story of the exodus is retold through the reading of the Haggadah. With its special foods, songs, and customs, the seder is the focal point of the Passover celebration and is traditionally a time of family gathering The name itself refers to the fact that God "passed over" the houses of the Jews when he set about slaying the firstborn sons of Egypt as the last of the ten plagues aimed at convincing Pharaoh to free the Jews. During Passover, Jews refrain from eating *chametz* – anything that contains leavened barley, wheat, rye, oats, and spelt – to commemorate the fact that the Jews leaving Egypt did not have time to let their bread rise. They also remove these foods and any food that has come in contact with them from their homes before the festival in an annual housecleaning, and use a separate set of Passover dishes that have never come into contact with chametz and are only used at this time of the year. *See also chametz*; Four Questions; Hagaddah; seder; seder plate.

perina (Russian) Duvet or comforter.

piechka (Russian) Stove, used for both heating and cooking.

Piłsudski, Marshal Józef (1867–1935) Leader of the Second Polish Republic from 1926 to 1935, Józef Piłsudski is considered to be a hero and as largely responsible for achieving Poland's independence in 1918 after more than a century of being partitioned by Russia, Austria and Prussia. Piłsudski's regime was notable for the improvement in the situation of ethnic minorities, including Poland's large Jewish population. He followed a policy of "state-assimilation" whereby citizens were judged not by their ethnicity but by their loyalty to the state. Many Polish Jews felt that his regime was key in keeping the antisemitic currents in Poland in check; many voted for him and actively participated in his political bloc. When he died in 1935, the quality of life of Poland's Jews deteriorated once again. Until his death, he also managed to keep both Hitler and Stalin at bay, resisting Germany's attempts to pressure Poland into an alliance against the USSR and extending a Soviet-Polish nonaggression treaty to 1945.

papiros (Russian) Cigarette.

pastuch (Russian) Shepherd.

progul (Russian) Absenteeism or truancy. In the USSR, being charged with absence from work without proper permission – which could only be obtained with a doctor's note verifying that the person had a temperature of at least 40 degrees Celsius – carried a sentence that could range from a substantial cut in pay to three months to one year hard labour in prison.

Red Army Day The holiday that honoured all those who served or were serving in the Soviet Union's armed forces. The date itself – February 23 – commemorates the first mass draft into the Red Army in 1918 during the Russian Civil War. The day was renamed "Defender of the Fatherland Day" in 1991 and is still celebrated in Russia, Ukraine and the former Soviet Republics.

Rosh Hashanah (Hebrew) New Year. Autumn holiday that marks the beginning of the Jewish year.

ruble (Russian) Unit of currency in the Soviet Union as well as in the Russian Federation today. The ruble was also the unit of currency in the pre-Soviet Russian Empire.

seder (Hebrew; literally: order) A ritual family meal celebrated on the first two nights of the eight day festival of Passover in the diaspora, and on the first night only in modern Israel. *See also* Passover.

seder plate Special plate containing six symbolic foods used by Jews during the Passover seder. Each item on the plate has special significance in the retelling of the story of the Jewish exodus from Egypt. A seventh symbolic item used during the meal – a stack of three matzos usually covered with decorative cloth – is placed on its own plate on the seder table. The six foods on the seder plate are *maror* (bitter herbs), which symbolize the bitterness of slavery in Egypt; *charoset* (sweet, brown-coloured mixture, traditionally made from apples, nuts and other ingredients), which symbolizes the mortar used by the Jewish slaves in Egypt; *karpas* (green vegetable), which is dipped into salt water at the beginning of the seder to represents the tears of the Jewish slaves; *z'roa* (roasted lamb, goat or chicken bone) and *beitzah* (hard-boiled egg), which both symbolize different sacrifices offered in the Temple in Jerusalem. *See also* Passover; seder.

Shabbat (Hebrew, in Yiddish, *Shabbes, Shabbos*) Sabbath. The weekly day of rest that for Jews begins on Friday at sundown and ends on Saturday at sundown. It is ushered in by the lighting of candles on Friday night and the recitation of blessings over wine – called Kiddush – and braided egg bread called challah; a day of celebration as well prayer, it is customary to eat three festive meals, attend synagogue services and refrain from doing any work or travelling.

shul (Yiddish) Synagogue or Jewish house of prayer.

shtiebl (Yiddish) Small, unadorned prayer room or prayer house furnished like synagogues but much more modestly. Most observant Jews in Eastern Europe prayed in *shtiebl*s on a daily basis; they attended services in a synagogue on holidays or sometimes on Shabbat.

siddur (Hebrew) Prayer book.

Simchat Torah (Hebrew; literally: rejoicing in the Torah) Jewish holiday that marks the conclusion of the annual cycle of readings from the Torah and the beginning of a new cycle. The holiday is a particularly joyous one, marked by singing and dancing with the Torah scrolls in synagogue and involvement of children in the synagogue service.

Soviet-Finnish War Also known as the Winter War; conflict that began on November 30, 1939, when the Soviets invaded Finland after the country had been ceded to the USSR by the Molotov-Ribbentrop Pact. Although the Soviet forces were in many aspects superior to the Finnish, the Finns were able to resist the invasion of their country with great success and for far longer than the Soviets had expected. Unable to get help from Britain and France, Finland signed the Moscow Peace Treaty on March 1940, ceding about 9 per cent of its pre-war territory and 20 per cent of its industrial capacity to the Soviet Union. Approximately 3,500 Finnish prisoners of war ended up in the USSR; 1,388 of them are known to have died while imprisoned.

sovkhoz (Russian, short for *Sovetskoye khozyaystvo*, meaning soviet farm) Usually translated as state farm, the term *sovkhoz* refers to a large, industrialized state-owned farm developed as part of Soviet collectivization policies of the 1930s; larger and different from a *kolkhoz*, a collective farm. *See also* collectivization; *kolkhoz.*

spekulant (Russian, plural: *spekulanty*) Speculator. In the USSR, free market activity was considered an anathema to both communist ideology and the centrally planned, state-controlled economy that were the cornerstones of the Soviet system. The intent to resell anything for profit – speculating – was a very serious crime, subject to Article 154 of the Soviet criminal code. A *spekulant* was considered to be "parasite," working in opposition to the "socially useful labour" that was the duty of every Soviet citizen, and therefore an enemy of the state.

stipenda (Russian) Scholarship.

Tekhnikum Soviet-era technical and vocational high school; a part of the Soviet mass-education system that focused on the "special middle education" of low-level industrial managers or those going into skilled trades and technical occupations.

tefillin (Hebrew) Phylacteries. Pair of black leather boxes containing scrolls of parchment inscribed with bible verses and worn by Jews on the arm and forehead at prescribed times of prayer as a symbol of the covenantal relationship with God.

traktory (Russian) Heavy shoes made from recycled tires, usually worn without socks.

ucha (Russian) Fish soup.

Treaty of Non-aggression between Germany and the USSR Colloquially known as the Molotov-Ribbentrop Pact for Soviet foreign minister Vyacheslav Molotov and German foreign minister Joachim von Ribbentrop, this treaty was signed on August 24, 1939. The main provisions of the pact stipulated that the two countries would not go to war with each other and that they would both remain neutral if either one was attacked by a third party. One of the key components of the treaty was the division of various independent countries – including Poland – into Nazi and Soviet spheres of influence. The Nazis breached the pact by launching a major offensive against the Soviet Union on June 22, 1941. It was these events that led to the occupations of Rokitno first by the Soviets and then by the Germans.

valenki (Russian) Felt boots.

volnye (Russian) Freed; released prisoners.

Volksdeutsche (German) The term used for ethnic Germans who lived outside Germany in Central and Eastern Europe. Prior to World War II, there were more than 10 million ethnic Germans living in these countries, some of whose families had been there for centuries. When the Nazis occupied these territories, they intended to reclaim the *Volksdeutsche* as Germans and strengthen their communities as a central part of creating the Nazis' ideal of a Greater Germany. Ethnic Germans were often given the choice to either to sign the *Volksliste*, the list of German people, and be regarded as traitors by their home countries, or not to sign and be treated as traitors to the "Germanic race" by the Nazi occupiers. After the collapse of Nazi Germany these people were persecuted by the post-war authorities in their home countries.

Warsaw Ghetto Uprising The largest single revolt by Jews during the Holocaust, the Warsaw Ghetto Uprising developed in response to the Nazis deportation of more than 275,000 ghetto inhabitants to slave-labour and death camps and the murder of another 10,000 of them between July and September 1942. When the Germans initiated the liquidation of the ghetto's remaining population of approximately 60,000 Jews by deporting them to the Treblinka death camp on April 19, 1943, about 750 organized ghetto fighters launched an insurrection. Despite some support from Jewish and Polish resistance organizations outside the ghetto, the poorly armed insurgents were crushed by the Germans after a month on May 16, 1943. More than 56,000 Jews were captured; about 7,000 were shot and the remainder were deported to death camps and concentration camps.

Yahrzeit (Yiddish) The commemoration of the anniversary of a Jewish person's death by the child, spouse, sibling or parent of the deceased. It is observed on the anniversary of the relative's death according to the Jewish caendar.

Yiddishkeit A term that denotes the "Jewishness" or "Jewish essence" of traditional Yiddish-speaking Jews in Eastern and Central Europe. Yiddishkeit usually refers to the popular culture or practices of Yiddish-speaking Jews – such as popular religious traditions, Eastern European Jewish food, Yiddish humour, shtetl life, and klezmer music – and also to a feeling of emotional attachment or identification with the Jewish people.

Yidl mitn Fidl (Yiddle with His Fiddle) A highly successful Yiddish-language film made in Poland in 1936 by Joseph Green starring New York–born Yiddish theatre, radio and television icon Molly Picon. Green immigrated to the US from Poland in 1924 and made four Yiddish films between 1935 and 1937 that captured life in the Jewish shtetls of Eastern Europe.

Young Pioneers The Young Pioneer Organization of the Soviet Union, also called the Lenin All-Union Pioneer Organization. A mass youth organization that served to instill communist ideology in children age ten to fifteen in the Soviet Union. Following their participation in the Young Pioneers, adolescents typically joined the Komsomol. *See also* Komsomol.

Zakliuchonye (Russian) Prisoners.

Maps & Photographs

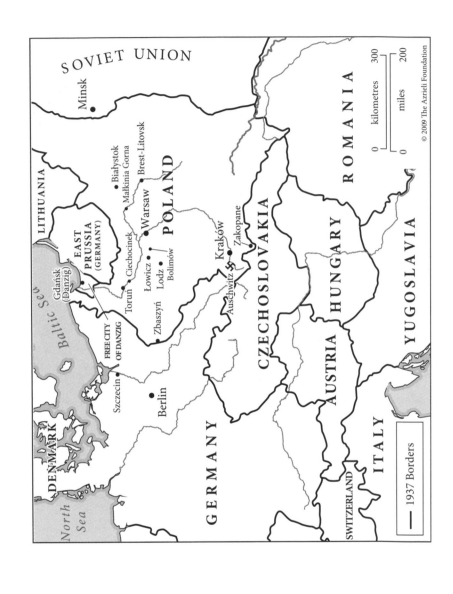

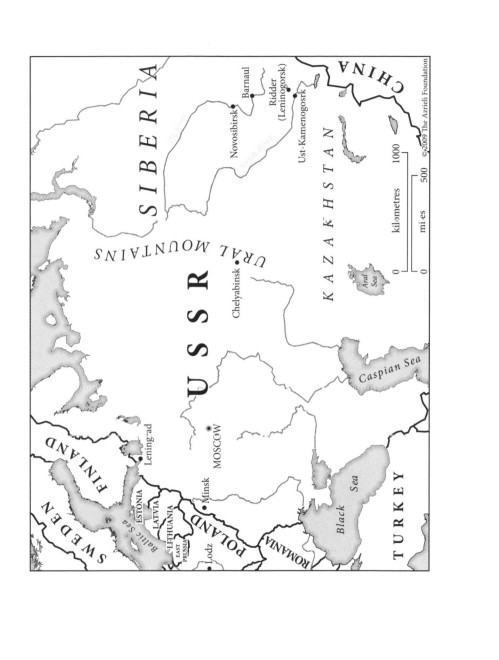

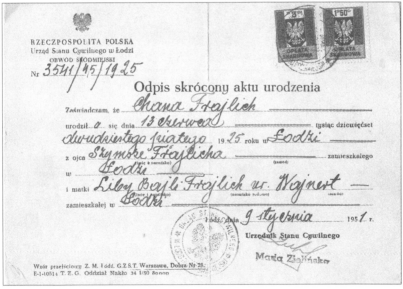

The last photograph, taken in Bolimów, Poland, that Ann Szedlecki received from her family in the Warsaw ghetto. Left to right: Ann's father, Shimshon Frajlich; Ann's mother, Liba Bayla Frajlich, holding her granddaughter, Miriam; Ann's sister, Manya; and her two aunts, Tauba and Sarah.

Ann's re-issued birth certificate, Lodz, 1951.

The street sign for Stary Rynek, the street where Ann was born.

A modern photograph of the courtyard at Stary Rynek No. 1, where Ann's family was living when she was born in 1925.

The street sign for Podrzeczna, where Ann's family moved in 1935.

A modern photograph of the tenement that was Podrzeczna No. 12 when Ann lived there as a child in Lodz.

A modern photograph of the bandstand in Helenów Park, Lodz.

A modern photograph of Public School No. 132 for Jewish Girls in Lodz.

A photograph of Ann when she was living in Siberia during the war.

1 Gienia Kaliner.

2 Pesach Kaliner.

3 A modern photograph of the house where Ann lived when she returned to Lodz after the war.

The sheared off wall where the Frajlich family's apartment building had stood on Polnocna before the war. This is what Ann found when she returned to Lodz in 1946.

Ann with her husband, Abraham Szedlecki, in Lodz, c1947.

Ann Szedlecki, Poland, c1949.

Ann Szedlecki on a visit to Israel in 1984.

Ann (left) with Gienia Kaliner Fogelbaum, Toronto.

Ann with her granddaughter Miriam, Toronto.

Ann in front of her exhibit at the Holocaust Education Centre in Toronto.

Ann's daughter, Lynda Kraar (right), with Lynda's daughters Miriam (left) and Yona.

Index

The Azrieli Foundation

The Azrieli Foundation was established in 1989 to realize and extend the philanthropic vision of David J. Azrieli, C.M., C.Q., MArch. The Foundation's mission is to support a wide spectrum of initiatives in education and research. The Azrieli Foundation is an active supporter of programs in the fields of Jewish education, the education of architects, scientific and medical research, and education in the arts. The Azrieli Foundation's many well-known initiatives include: the Holocaust Survivor Memoirs Program, which collects, preserves, publishes and distributes the written memoirs of survivors in Canada; the Azrieli Institute for Educational Empowerment, an innovative program successfully working to keep at-risk youth in school; and the Azrieli Fellows Program, which promotes academic excellence and leadership on the graduate level at Israeli universities. Programs sponsored and supported are located in Canada, Israel and the United States.

Israel and Golda Koschitzky Centre for Jewish Studies

In 1989, York University established Canada's first interdisciplinary research centre in Jewish studies. Over the years, the Israel and Golda Koschitzky Centre for Jewish Studies has earned national and international acclaim for its dynamic approach to teaching and research. While embracing Jewish culture and classical study in all its richness, the Centre also has a distinctly modern core, and a strong interest in the study of the Canadian Jewish experience. York was the Canadian pioneer in the study of the Holocaust. The Centre maintains its strong commitment to the study of the Holocaust through the research, teaching, and community involvement of its faculty, its graduate diploma program in Advanced Hebrew and Jewish Studies, and its unique program of Holocaust and anti-racist education – developed in cooperation with the Centre for German and European Studies – for Canadian, German and Polish education students.